Life Management for Busy Women

Elizabeth George

HARVEST HOUSE™ PUBLISHERS

EUGENE, OREGON

Cover by Terry Dugan Design, Minneapolis, Minnesota

Acknowledgments

As always, thank you to my dear husband, Jim George, M.Div., Th.M., for your able assistance, guidance, suggestions, and loving encouragement on this project.

Life Management for Busy Women
Copyright © 2002 by Elizabeth George
Published by Harvest House Publishers
Eugene, Oregon 97402

Library of Congress Cataloging-in-Publication Data
George, Elizabeth, 1944-
    Life management for busy women / Elizabeth George.
        p. cm.
  Includes bibliographical references.
    ISBN 0-7369-0191-4 (pbk.)
    1. Christian women—Religious life. I. Title.
    BV4527 .G4594 2002
    248.8'43—dc21
                                                           2002004548

Printed in the United States of America

02   03   04   05   06   07   08   09   10   11   / BP-MS /   10 9 8 7 6 5 4 3 2 1

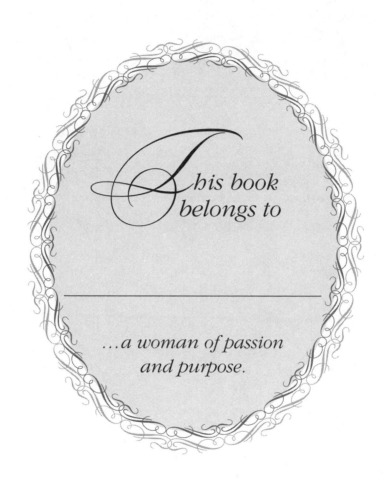

This book belongs to

_____

...a woman of passion and purpose.

Contents

An Invitation to...
a Life of Passion and Purpose

Do you ever wonder what the purpose of your life is? And do you ever feel like life is piling up on you faster than you can push your way forward? That your days are doomed before dawn? That you'll never get it all done? That there has to be more to life than this?

Well, we can both thank God that there is hope for our hearts and answers to our heart-cries. Our lives were created by God...and He knows *what* His purposes for us are and *how* He wants us to live them out. Indeed, our years, our days, and even our minutes(!) belong to Him.

I'm so glad that God has brought us together through this book. As you and I, two extremely busy women, head into this book about a passion for managing a life of purpose and some of the disciplines needed to fuel such a life, I want to do several things. I want...

- To bring you God's guidelines for seven major areas of a woman's life.

- To direct you to the specific disciplines that will help you manage each of these seven areas of your life.

- To list a handful of *how-to's* so you can make progress right away on managing your time and your life.

- To point you to the beauty—and power—of a life lived according to God's principles and purposes.

There's no doubt that the forever principles shared in this book can sculpt and remold your life. (Believe me, they ignited a fire not only in my soul but also in my entire approach to each day and its 1440 minutes!)

I also invite you to take advantage of the supplemental *Life Management for Busy Women Growth and Study Guide.* This helpful volume will propel you down the path toward better stewardship of your time and your life. Its practical exercises will assist you (and others in a group setting) in faithfully following God's blueprint for your life as His woman...a woman with a passion for living for Him!

My desire for you as you read this book is that you will walk in wisdom and make the most of your time and your life (Colossians 4:5 and Ephesians 5:15). May we remember that we live life one day at a time...yet we are living for eternity in that one day!

Part I

At the Heart
of It All

Managing Your
Spiritual Life

Chapter 1

Developing a Passion
for God's Word

But those who wait on the LORD
shall renew their strength;
they shall mount up with wings like eagles,
they shall run and not be weary,
they shall walk and not faint.
—ISAIAH 40:31

As a busy woman, your natural tendency at the sound of the alarm each morning is probably to hit the floor running (like me!). And for many women, each day also includes hitting the road at some point as they head off to a job. At the dreaded sound of the alarm (or of a crying baby!), we are so often tempted to emote, "Oh, no! Another day! I have so much to do!" The blare coming from your clock reminds you (once again!) that you are faced with a life full of responsibilities.

And if we look a little deeper into our hearts, we also find thoughts like these—"I'll never get it all done...especially if I take time out of my hectic schedule to read my Bible and pray!"

But, dear one, the exact opposite is true for you and me as God's busy women, for it was our Lord Himself who said, "*Without* Me you can do nothing" (John 15:5).

Like an Eagle

By contrast, the Bible teaches us that *with* Him we can "mount up with wings like eagles" (Isaiah 40:31). Can you imagine...soaring through your pressured days like an eagle?! Every morning Jim (my wonderful husband) and I watch and wait for "our" white-headed, white-tailed, American bald eagle to fly by our home in Washington. And sure enough, today at 5:47 A.M. (right on schedule) it flew at eye level past the window where we sit each day to write. The sight is so magnificent that we celebrate each and every time our eagle graces us with its presence. Our eagle sightings have given me a first-hand visual aid for understanding Isaiah's imagery of strength and endurance.

Since realizing that Jim and I have our own private eagle (or two), I've learned a lot more about eagles. For instance, an eagle...

> ...has a wingspan of up to seven feet (how majestic!)
>
> ...flies higher than almost any other bird, up to 10,000 feet (how awesome!)
>
> ...glides easily at up to 2400 feet altitude (oh, for the ability to rise above life's demands and difficulties!)
>
> ...moves up to 150 miles an hour (and oh, for the ability to speed through our daily work!) and
>
> ...can carry objects equal to its body weight (no task is too daunting!).

With such grandeur available to our imagination it's clear that even with our multitude of responsibilities, we must be women who wait on the Lord. In spite of the busy-ness of life, you and I must learn to look to Him each new morning. We must realize that *life* management is really *spiritual* life management. So we must pay attention to a handful of daily disciplines that are sure to ignite in us a passion for the Lord and equip us for living out His plan each day...and for life!

Three Small Steps

Here's a little three-step method that helps us tend to first things first...no matter how busy we are.

1. *Time* is first on the list. Our time is always well spent when we spend it looking to the Lord through His Word. You and I must acknowledge this truth and accept it for life. We must embrace the challenge to cultivate the discipline of daily time in the Bible into our daily routine. What time?

2. *First* time. Aim at giving the first minutes of each day to the reading of God's Word. Proverbs 3:9 instructs you and me to "Honor the LORD with your possessions, and with the firstfruits of all your increase." Then comes the promise—"so your barns will be filled with plenty, and your vats will overflow with new wine" (verse 10). This proverb is speaking of the blessings that follow the offering of a tithe to God of the first crops from the harvest.

   But the same results occur in the spiritual realm. We are blessed in our spirit and in our practical life when we make it a point to give God the first portion

11

of time from the harvest of each fresh new day, of each new measure of 1440 minutes.

3.   *Early* time. David wrote these expressive words from the core of his heart—"O God, You are my God; early will I seek You; my soul thirsts for You" (Psalm 63:1). Many of the great heroes of the faith sincerely sought communion with God early and earnestly in their day. For instance,

—Abraham rose up early in the morning and went to the place where he met with the Lord (Genesis 19:27).

—David wrote of morning worship with these utterances: "My voice You shall hear in the morning, O LORD; in the morning I will direct it to You, and I will look up" (Psalm 5:3). I particularly love the translation that reads, "at dawn I hold myself in readiness for you, I watch for you."[1]

—And our Lord Jesus rose up early, while it was still night, literally a long while before daylight, to converse in solitude with His heavenly Father (Mark 1:35).

Three small steps. And three simple steps any woman can take! A *time,* the *first* time, and an *early* time. As I'm thinking back to our eagle and its daily visit, I realize that it comes for a purpose—to get food for the day. And it comes as the *first* act of its day, taking care of first things first, the priority of ensuring sustenance, nutrition, and energy. And it comes *early*—at the first hint of daybreak, as soon as it can see, at 5:47 A.M.

And, my precious, passionate, reading friend, the eagle's discipline has got to become ours, too! You and I need the spiritual food only the Word of God can provide...and that takes *time*. And we need to gather that food *first* thing each day, before life presents its daily demands on our hours and our energy. And we need to do it *early*, before the rush and clamor of the day begin. Otherwise, just as the eagle knows, it's too late. The brief opening for obtaining the prized and necessary food for the day is gone. The sun rises, the heat is on, and other predators come to compete for our precious time and energy. Gone is the small window of a handful of minutes that was ours for the taking...when we were alone...when all was quiet.

So often people ask me how I have been able to accomplish so much writing in such a short time. It's these three small steps that I have faithfully taken for the past 30 years that have helped to develop a personal reservoir of God's Word at the heart of my life. And now, in God's timing, His principles that have guided my life have come flowing out in service to His women.

Time, first time, *early* time. I personally can't say enough (and strongly enough!) about this key that is at the heart of all that we dream and yearn to be for the Lord. It's such a simple formula. And it sounds so easy, doesn't it? And it can be yours, too. But as you and I well know, making time for anything of value always requires a hard commitment to discipline! So let's look at some of the benefits of such a discipline. They should inspire us to seek time with the Lord.

The Power of God's Word

Behind the passionate life of every passionate saint is a passion for God and His Word. And time in God's Word is

13

how we tap into the power it makes available to us (the power that assists us in mounting up with wings like an eagle!). I hope you sense that passion in my life. And I hope you are desiring it for yours as well.

I've spent many a Sunday morning listening to Jim preach from his favorite book of the Bible, 2 Timothy. It's a short—but passionate—letter written by the apostle Paul to Timothy, Paul's disciple and a "man of God." It's also a letter that contains a straightforward, heart-to-heart, hard-line call to Timothy to live a hardened, tough-as-nails, disciplined life. Why? So that Timothy could glorify God with his life and his service (you and I want that too, don't we?)…and so that he could stand up to the trials of life (and you and I need that too, don't we?).

Toward the end of his epistle, Paul paints a masterful picture of what the Word of God is and what it does for those who make it a part of their active lives. Hear now from Paul (and a few other writers of Scripture). And walk through a few of the characteristics of God's powerful Word:

> All Scripture is given by inspiration of God, and is profitable for doctrine, for reproof, for correction, for instruction in righteousness, that the man of God may be complete, thoroughly equipped for every good work (2 Timothy 3:16-17).

God's Word is the heart of God—Would you like to know God's thoughts, to hear His heart, to have a little of the heavenly be a part of your everyday life? Then read God's Word. *Every*thing that God wants to say to you is recorded in your Bible…straight from His heart to yours. It is God-breathed,

14

inspired by Him, and comes from Him (2 Timothy 3:16). And it contains the counsel of the Lord and the thoughts of His heart to all generations (Psalm 33:11). So, as the psalmist so passionately invites you, "Oh, *taste* and see that the LORD is good" (Psalm 34:8).

God's Word is a good use of your time—You never have to worry about wasting your time if it's being spent reading God's good and useful and helpful Word. For instance,

> If you are impatient, sit down quietly and commune with Job. If you are strong-headed, read of Moses and Peter. If you are weak-kneed, look at Elijah. If there is no song in your heart, listen to David sing. If you are a politician, read Daniel. If you are getting sordid, read Isaiah. If your heart is chilly, read of the beloved disciple, John. If your faith is low, read Paul. If you are getting lazy, watch James. If you are losing sight of the future, read in Revelation of the promised land. In joy and sorrow, in health and in sickness, in poverty and in riches, in every condition of life, God has [something] stored up in His Word for you.[2]

So, do you need wisdom? You'll find it in the Bible. Do you need encouragement? It, too, lies on the sacred pages of Scripture. Do you need strength? Just reading God's Word infuses you with strength—His strength—for today and hope—His hope—for tomorrow. Just pause, pick up your cherished volume of the Bible, and do the best thing you can do with your time—behold the Word of the Lord! As

Paul explains, all Scripture is indeed "profitable" (2 Timothy 3:16).

God's Word teaches you (2 Timothy 3:16)—Don't be like the women various Bible translations describe as "weak-willed" or "gullible" or "silly" who were "always learning and never able to come to the knowledge of the truth" (verses 6-7). As women with a passion for God, you and I must grow in our knowledge of the Word. There's no reason for our faith to be anything less than firmly grounded. Let God's Word teach you doctrine, theology, and truth—truth about Jesus Christ, truth about the Christian faith, and truth about how God wants you to live your life. Again, just read your Bible!

God's Word reproves you (2 Timothy 3:16 again). Speaking of power, the Bible refers to itself as "living and *powerful*, and sharper than any two-edged sword." And it describes its action in our heart as "piercing even to the division of soul and spirit, and of joints and marrow," and as "a discerner of the thoughts and intents of the heart" (Hebrews 4:12). Therefore, when you pore over the pages of Scripture, it speaks straight to your heart. It points to behaviors or attitudes or practices that don't match up with God's standard for His people. As Martin Luther put it,

> The Bible is alive, it speaks to me;
> it has feet, it runs after me;
> it has hands, it lays hold on me.[3]

God's Word corrects, mends, and instructs you (2 Timothy 3:16, yet again)—Have you been reproved? Well, cheer up. God's Word also has the power to mend you and move you forward. After you've fallen and failed, God's Word picks you up, brushes you off, straightens you out, and builds you up until you are restored to the condition God has in mind for you. We're seeking to manage our life *God's way*...and His Word is constantly correcting and resetting the direction of our lives, preparing us for living out His plan and purpose in future service.

God's Word equips you (2 Timothy 3:17)—What is it you need to do today? Next week? Next year? What tasks, roles, services, and ministries do you desire to manage and live out excellently? Whatever it is, God's Word will more than adequately equip you to perform the work and the ministry God has for you at home and in the church. God's Word will give you the power to meet the demands of serving the Lord and living in righteousness.

God's Word guides you—Have you ever been camping and had to walk at night from your car to your campsite or from one building to the next? Then you know how dark the path can be...and how indispensable and helpful and necessary your flashlight was! Even though its beam probably only lit the area where you would take your next step, that was enough for you to walk safely.

That's how God's Word guides you. Switching from Paul to the psalmist, we learn that God's Word is a lamp to our feet and a light to our path (Psalm 119:105). Its powerful beacon illuminates at least our next step, our next decision, our next activity. There's no need for you to ever stumble through life or miss your way...*if* God's Word is implemented to light up the next portion of the path. Be sure you turn to the Bible to show you the right way, to help you to avoid the wrong way, and to manage your life *God's* way!

God's Word cheers you—Is joy missing from your life? Are these sad days for you, dear one? Are there sorrows you must bear? Then look to the sustenance of God's Word. That's what the prophet Jeremiah did when he was in despair. And then He reported, "Your words were found, and I ate them, and Your word was to me the joy and rejoicing of my heart" (Jeremiah 15:16). What a joyous blessing!

As I write about this truth, my heart is sad. Jim and I are just home from Manhattan, New York, home from welcoming our daughter's baby, Matthew, into this world... born just hours before the terrorist attack on the World Trade Center on September 11. The two weeks we were delayed in Manhattan were sad ones—and our hearts remain heavy. So where did (and do!) Jim and I go for joy at such a time? To the Word of God. Indeed, we rushed to it! The same joy and rejoicing of heart—along with God's peace and perspective—is available to you when grief and gloom are a part of each day.

Looking at Life

As we step into our journey together through this book about managing our lives, we are immediately forced to realize that God has already given us the map for our venture. And that map is God's Word, the Bible. It teaches us, reproves us, corrects us, mends us, instructs us, equips us, guides us, and cheers us along the way. What more could we need as we trek through life?!

And yet we've all heard testimonies like those below shared by Christians who said things about their journeys such as,

> I wandered off the path...
> I became like the prodigal son...

> I fell away from the Lord…
> I got sidetracked in sin…
> I lost my first love…
> I strayed from the truth…
> I made some wrong decisions…
> I went off the deep end…
> I got in with the wrong crowd…

I always wonder, *What happened?* How does someone wander off the path? How does a prodigal become a prodigal? How do we become sidetracked? How does one lose his or her first love, stray from the truth, begin making wrong decisions and mistakes? What leads up to going off the deep end, leaving the flock of God, choosing a lifestyle of wallowing in the mire, and eating the husks meant for pigs?

We both know what happened, don't we? Somehow, at some time, for some reason, God's Word took a secondary place to other pursuits. The lesser choices were made regarding how time was spent, until time was not taken each day to develop a passion for knowing and following God's plan.

Beloved, at the heart of a woman seeking to live out God's plan for her life is a passion for God's Word. And when we fail to purposefully and willfully develop this passion, we begin to spend our precious time and days on lesser pursuits…which can lead to wandering off the path of God's purpose for our life and out of His will.

Your life and living out God's plan and purpose for your life are at stake. And the lives of your loved ones—your marriage partner and your dear children, who are meant to be the next generation of Christians—are also at stake. And your witness at work and in the neighborhood is at stake. Why?

Because what you do and don't do to manage your life doesn't only affect you. It affects everyone and everything!

So I'm calling you to do whatever it takes to develop a passion for God's Word and the disciplines that will fuel in your heart an intense passion for the Bible. As someone has well said,

> The study of God's Word
> for the purpose of discovering God's will
> is the secret discipline
> which has formed the greatest characters.[4]

Now, are you ready to consider some of the disciplines that assist us in getting into God's Word? Then let's read on about getting down to those disciplines.

Chapter 2

Ten Disciplines for Developing a Passion for God's Word

*I have treasured the words of His mouth
more than my necessary food.*
—JOB 23:12

"Discipline is demanded of the athlete to win a game. Discipline is required for the captain running his ship. Discipline is needed for the pianist to practice for the concert."[1] And, dear reading sister, discipline is called for in developing a passion for God's Word.

In our quest to kindle such a transforming passion, we've savored some of the sweet blessings that are ours when we indulge and delight in God's Word. And hopefully by now you have made a commitment to take the three small steps that help to give the Scriptures a reigning place in your heart and in your life and in each new busy day—*time, first* time, and *early* time.

Now I want us to consider ten disciplines we must embed into our daily lives that will further ignite our hearts and souls. As we noted above, discipline is called for in developing a passion for God's Word.

Ten Disciplines for Developing
a Passion for God's Word

1. *Refuse to miss a day.* Make your first discipline a decision to be faithful in just one thing—in spending some portion of your day reading your Bible. Make your first discipline an attempt at not missing a single day. God's Word is at the heart of a woman—even a busy woman!—who is passionate about her relationship with Him.

Here's how one of the Bible's great men of faith viewed God's Word. In the midst of just about every kind of suffering known to mankind, Job declared, "I have treasured the words of His mouth more than my necessary food" (Job 23:12). This is quite a statement! Very few of us ever miss a meal. And Job is showing us that God's Word should hold a higher priority for our souls than our necessary food holds for our body. This grieving man, having lost all, cherished God's Word more than his daily food.

Let me tell you about a woman who "got it" when it came to the discipline of time in God's Word. At the time I met Donna, she was on the staff of the Campus Crusade for Christ ministry. And Donna took me, just a fledgling, under her wing and got me off to a good start as a Christian. She did a terrific job impressing upon me the need for a consistent, daily time in the Bible. And, I might add, she did it sweetly and casually as she talked to me in low, earnest tones while cooking an omelet for us to share. That was our topic for the day as we sat in her kitchen sharing physical food and sharing about a Christian woman's need for spiritual food.

To help me with this new discipline, I began using a "Quiet Times Calendar" (see pages 240-41) that required that I color on or shade in the spaces provided for each day

22

when I actually had a quiet time. The goal when using this calendar is to form a solid line (like the mercury of a thermometer) as you read your Bible day after day…seeking to never miss a day. Once again, the adage is true—one picture is worth a thousand words! Still, these many years later, all I ever have to do is look at that chart and I know—at a glance—how I'm doing. I either see the "thermometer" look (a solid line), the "Morse code" look (dot, dot, dash, dot, dot, dash), or the "measles" look (here a dot, there a dot, everywhere a dot, dot).

Now, how do you think *your* Quiet Times Calendar would look? Are you getting closer to developing the discipline of refusing to miss a day?

2.   *Pray as you approach God's Word.* That's what the psalmist did. He prayed, "Open my eyes, that I may see wondrous things from Your law." And in the next breath, he pleaded, "Do not hide Your commandments from me" (Psalm 119:18-19). Ask the Holy Spirit to illuminate the Word of God to your soul and your spirit. Ask Him to assist you in understanding the living Word of God. Do as Solomon advised and cry out for knowledge and lift up your voice for understanding (Proverbs 2:3).

3.   *Consume God's Word in various ways.* Don't stop at reading your Bible. Play teaching tapes and videos, too. Memorize and meditate on specific Bible verses. Place Scripture verses at strategic places throughout the house (or on your computer and at your workplace on the job). Hum through the words and melodies of the great hymns of the faith and songs of praise and worship. Aim at making the meditations of your heart acceptable in the sight of the Lord

(Psalm 19:14). And aim at the saturation of your heart, soul, and mind with the Word of God.

And here's an inspiring note on memorizing Scripture—Dawson Trotman, the founder of the Navigators ministry, set a goal as a new Christian to memorize one verse a day. On his third spiritual birthday, he recited over 1000 verses from memory...word perfectly! Now, couldn't you memorize just *one* verse a week?

I know you're busy. But do you realize that not one of these Scripture-absorbing activities requires your time? They only require your heart and mind. *As* you go about your busy life and your duties and your chores and your work, you hum (at least in your heart!), you listen, you memorize, you meditate. All this exercise of consuming God's Word in various ways requires is a decision and a little preparation. We must, must, *must* make...and take...time to be in God's Word. Why? Because in the Bible we find *every*thing we need to guide and energize our lives, to keep us on track so that we live out God's plan.

4. *Find a rhythm or a pattern that fits your lifestyle.* I'll die teaching (and attempting to practice!) *time, first* time, and *early* time. And there are two reasons for this personal preference. The first is my desire to go through each busy day without the burden of guilt that hangs over me when I haven't gotten to my Bible reading. In my soul (and on my schedule!), time in God's Word is something I need to do, want to do, and must do...and there's a cloud hanging over my bright day until I get to that special time with God. There's an unsettledness in everything I do because I know—both from my to-do list and from my heart—that there's something I need to do, some duty left undone. Therefore, sooner is better than later!

And the second reason is my desire for wisdom and strength—*God's* wisdom and strength—throughout my day. I desperately desire His image stamped upon the life I am called by Him to live each day. And I need His advice for managing the day...and its crises...and its busy-ness! I need His input. His direction. His guidance. His encouragement. Time in the Scriptures (and again, the sooner the better!) turns my heart's gaze toward God and makes my days—and my management—markedly better.

It's up to you to find the time for reading your Bible that fits your lifestyle. But do find it so that you won't use a busy life as an excuse like this woman did—

> I am a young mom and I homeschool, so I keep busy. I've used this as an excuse in my relationship with God. I want to be a woman after God's own heart, so I have committed to pray and establish a more meaningful quiet time and to seek greater spiritual growth.

And, by the way, *bravo* to this wonderful young mom for making a serious decision, a decision that's at the heart of it all!

5. *Be a woman of one Book—the Book.* There are many books you and I can spend time reading. Some are bad, some are good, and some are better. But our reading calls for discipline. At least two disciplines will put us on the right path as we fuel our passion for God.

First, make it a rule to read what honors God's standards and glorifies Him.

And second, if you only have time to read one book, make sure that book is *the* Book, the Bible. I have friends who even make it a discipline to read the Bible *before* they read anything else each day. No newspaper, no devotional reader, no instructive book, and no fiction until their Bible is read. It was said of John Wesley, the brilliant founder of Methodism and one who was heralded as a shining example of consecrated intellect, that he was a "man of one Book."[2]

Dear one, read your Bible. Become addicted to your Bible. Love your Bible. Indeed, cherish it. I was so touched while reading of the death of theologian Francis Schaeffer to learn that he lay on his deathbed holding his Bible to his chest with one hand and stroking it with the other. Too weak to hold his Bible open for reading, Dr. Schaeffer clutched and caressed it. You see, he was a man of one Book—*the* Book.

6. *Be accountable.* Thomas Edison made it his practice to first announce his intentions on a given project...and then get into the laboratory, get busy, and make the announcement become a reality! So...take a page out of Edison's book. Declare your intentions to those who care for you most and are willing to check up on you and "hold your feet to the fire," so to speak.

Who would such a person be? Christian friends. And Christian mentors. Maybe even your husband (if he wants that role—be sure and ask him first!). There are three general kinds of acquaintances in life—those who pull you down, those who pull you along, and those who pull you up. Obviously someone you would be accountable to for any element of spiritual growth would be one who pulls you along, who is like-minded, who is moving toward the same zeal in Christ you are. Such a friend would most certainly want to help you grow. And the same is true of one who pulls you up, who is a step (or two!) ahead of you, who inspires you and/or is willing to disciple and mentor you to even greater growth. Ask for accountability...and then set about to do your part to make your desire to be a woman with a daily passion for God's Word a reality.

And while you're asking for accountability, be sure you ask for your friends' much-needed prayer on your behalf. And don't forget to add your own prayers for dedication and faithfulness to your new disciplines.

7. *Beat the family.* Does this sound strange? What I mean is to aim at getting up before your family gets up. (Now, would it sound any better if I said, "Beat the family up"?)

As you take time via a personal quiet time to tune your heart strings to heaven, then—amazingly!—your "tune" is sweeter when your husband and children get up. And it's also sweeter as you whistle or hum a happy tune while going about your work. In your quiet time you've touched, perhaps in the Gospels, the Savior's life...and His life has once again touched yours. You've poured out your heart's concerns, perhaps through the Psalms, and you, like their writers, rise up better, strengthened for one more day, at peace, content, ready to focus on others and serve them for Christ's sake. With God's help and fresh fortitude, your day is undaunting as you face its challenges. Reminders from the Old Testament of God's care for His people down through the ages will arm you. Exhortations from the authors of the New Testament epistles to "stand strong," to "fight the good fight," to "walk the worthy walk"...for just one more day will strengthen you. We both know that our day takes on a whole new flavor when we've read God's Word first. So why not give your family (and/or your workmates) the blessing of God's divine influence on your life?

8.   *Teach your children.* John Ruskin, British educator and nineteenth-century art critic and Christian reformer, attributed the molding of his character to his mother's influence. He said, "She forced me to learn daily long chapters of the Bible by heart. To that discipline and patient, accurate resolve I owe not only much of my general power of taking pains, but of the best part of my taste for literature."[3] Yes, we set aside time so that *we* may take in God's Word…but we must also set aside time to ensure that our *children* do the same! It's a must…and it's yet another discipline we must be passionate about.

I know this discipline takes time out of an already-packed schedule. But this is time you must give if you are to fulfill God's command (Deuteronomy 6:7) to you as a Christian mother to teach the law of the Lord diligently to your little ones (and big ones, too). And don't worry—that time will be available once we order the activities of our lives with godly perspective.

Wouldn't you agree that a Bible time with the children God has given you is more important than the trip to the grocery store (which we somehow manage to faithfully fit in)…than the trip to the beauty shop (which, again, no matter how busy we are, we are able to miraculously fit in!)…than another trip on-line that strangely eats up our minutes (and even *hours!*) and our day's good intentions…than another trip to the mall, to a friend's house, etc.?

Amazingly, no matter how busy we are, *some* things manage to work their way into the crowded scene. So, as you think about first things first—God's Word first—think about it being first in your children's lives too. Make it a passion!

9. *Purpose to get up.* For most of us there's only one way to enjoy *time, first* time, and *early* time with God, and that's to set the alarm. Surely, any woman with any passion for anything makes sure she gets up to enjoy that passion! Save your sleeping-in for special days or for a reward for strenuous work finally finished. (Even then your burning passion may not allow you to sleep in!)

10. *Aim for more time.* Two good principles for determining the amount of time you spend reading your Bible are:

> *Something is better than nothing*
> and
> *Always aim for more.*

I can guarantee you that once you discipline yourself to meet regularly with God for *some* time, you'll become like David in Psalm 63—you'll hunger and thirst for *more* time with the Lord. Truly His Word is sweeter than honey and the honeycomb (Psalm 19:10).

And here's another principle from Donna, the brave woman who took me on as a disciple. Donna shared with me that she did not allow herself to spend more time in any personal activity (she specifically mentioned exercising and crafts) each day than she spent in the Word of God. Of course, as she discipled me, that principle was passed on to me and became a part of my life, too. And now it's my turn to pass it on to you!

Which brings us to Susanna Wesley, the mother of John Wesley, who wrote,

> I will tell you what rule I observed...when I was young, and too much addicted to childish diversions, which was this—Never to spend more time in mere recreation in one day than I spend in private religious devotions.[4]

I must warn you, if you get serious about this discipline, it will change your life—your schedule, your priorities, your focus, your perspective, and your interests. Beware...the ground is rumbling!

And how would such a discipline work for a woman who spends the bulk of her day at a job? Well, I would say that such a woman dare not go out into the world without spiritual preparation (and the more the better!). And even if she is going to work in a Christian organization, her work—anywhere and everywhere and in all things—is done unto the Lord. The goal is always to do our work—whether in a busy home or in a busy office or at the church—God's way and in His power. And that, beloved, requires spending time with Him. Time looking to Him. Time in prayer. Time in the Word. Lots of time! We simply must manage our busy days to ensure the discipline of time, time, and more time in these basic spiritual pursuits. For truly, they are at the heart of it all, at the heart of discovering and living out God's plan with passion and purpose.

Looking at Life

I know I've said a lot of things in this chapter on setting a few important disciplines for our lives in motion. Probably too many things! But, dear one, beloved and precious sister, words fail me in trying to reach across these pages to your heart. If you are God's child through Jesus Christ, you are a *spiritual* being. You were dead and are now alive in Christ. He gave birth to you—you've been born again! So, like any baby, you *must* grow. You *must* nurture your spiritual life and your spiritual health. And you *must* have the regular intake of spiritual food.

Let me tell you about Jim's mother, a saint of a mother-in-law. Lois had always read her Bible, served her family, and ministered in her church. But the happy days of hearth, home, and family soon took on the truth of author Edith Schaeffer's astute observation—"Life is a mountain climb to the very end!"[5] As Lois aged and suffered the deaths of two husbands, she increasingly read *more* of her Bible. She also devoured Bible-teaching tapes. She couldn't be at church enough to soak in her pastor's expounding of God's Word. Plus, she read Christian books with a voracious hunger.

Yes, there were her beloved devotional books and the inspiring biographies of the cloud of witnesses who had gone before her. But as the years went on, Lois read books on topics that were steadily heavier—books on theology, treatises on the nature and Person of God, and whole volumes of commentaries on the books of the Bible. As the decades slipped by, and the mountain climb of her life grew steeper and steeper, Lois, too, grew and grew in her knowledge of God's Word...until it was her constant diet as she fought her battle with cancer and finally slipped into the presence of the One she had loved supremely without seeing.

We can be sure there were days in Lois's 76 years when it was her heart's delight to turn to God's Word. And we can be sure there were days, too, when she did so because it was the right thing to do...and she knew it...and when it required determination and a decision to do it. Beloved, that's the way it is with a discipline—any discipline. You do it because it is what you need to do and are supposed to do and because it is the right thing to do. You do it because it contributes to and propels you toward what you want to be and do...and in our case, that is becoming women with a passion for God. And then...somehow...the duty of the discipline turns into sheer delight and we reap the blessings of a priceless, tender relationship with the Lord a thousandfold.

So, my companion-on-the-path-to-a-disciplined-life, a life managed with passion and purpose, where are you on life's road, on the mountain climb? What must you do? How will you begin? What first steps will you take? What will you do to not only avoid the unlovely and uncomfortable consequences of neglecting this all-encompassing, life-sustaining, life-directing (and life-changing!) discipline of the Christian life, but to indulge and delight yourself in the heavenly manna of God's Word?

Or, how will you increase and enhance the disciplines you already have in place? An athlete works out to sustain the strength already gained *and* to increase that strength for even greater feats and victories. And it's no different for you and me as women with a passion for God and for developing the disciplines that nurture this all-important relationship with God. As the demands in life go up, the intake of God's Word must go up so that the *harder* victories are won, until our ultimate victory of seeing our Lord face to face is realized.

Why not make the "rules" on the next page yours so that your days of climbing your mountain are sweeter and more hallowed?

Rules for Daily Life

Begin the day with God
Kneel down to Him in prayer;
Lift up thy heart to His abode,
And seek His love to share.

Open the book of God
And read a portion there;
That it may hallow all thy thoughts,
And sweeten all thy care.

Go through the day with God
Whate'er thy work may be;
Where'er thou art—at home, abroad,
He still is near to thee.

Converse in mind with God
Thy spirit heavenward raise:
Acknowledge every good bestowed,
And offer grateful praise.

Conclude the day with God
Thy sins to Him confess;
Trust in the Lord's atoning blood,
And plead His righteousness.

Lie down at night with God
Who gives His servants sleep;
And when thou tread'st the vale of death,
He will thee guard and keep.[6]

Chapter 3

Developing a Passion for Prayer

My voice You shall hear in the morning, O LORD; in the
morning I will direct it to You, and I will look up.
—PSALM 5:3

Whenever I teach on the spiritual life and the disciplines
that assist us in our desire to draw nearer to God, I like to
share this thought from John Flavel, a seventeenth-century
English clergyman who loved to teach and write about practical religion and piety:

> Observed duties maintain our credit, but
> secret duties maintain our life.

Certainly, as we've been learning, the reading and study
of God's Word is a *secret duty* that maintains our life. And,
beloved, so is prayer. Prayer is one more privilege—and
responsibility...and *secret duty!*—we have as Christians. It
is a privilege because of our relationship with God as His
children. And it is a responsibility and a duty because of the
many commands in Scripture that call us to a life of faithful
prayer.

Our Call to Prayer

No one could ever read the Bible and not notice its emphasis on prayer! From the opening pages of the Bible to its closing chapters, the men and women of faith are seen (and heard!) crying out to God. Indeed, whole prayers are recorded for us word for word.

In the Bible God tells us to call unto Him (Jeremiah 33:3), to ask of Him (James 1:5), to seek Him (Matthew 7:7). He also tells us to withdraw from others and to enter into our "closet," a secret chamber, a room or a place alone, and to pray to our Father in secret (Matthew 6:6 KJV).

I'm sure you can think of many more commands to pray that come to us from God Himself through His Word. For now, though, let's consider five feats prayer accomplishes in our heart and life.

The first is more of a reality than a feat—*prayer is a privilege*. Prayer is one way we commune with the God of the universe. He's our Sovereign. He's our Father. And, beloved, He's our Friend. I meet so many women who are lonely. But just think…when there is no one for you to talk to—no one present, no husband, no friend, no one who seems to care or understand, no one to listen to you—there is always God! Just think…the ears of the Creator of the world—the One who can do anything!—are open to your prayers (1 Peter 3:12). And just think…your Friend who sticks closer than a brother is *always* available to you and there for you (Proverbs 18:24). Truly, He is the One who will never leave you or forsake you (Hebrews 13:5). What a privilege we have to be able to link up with Him via prayer!

Next, *prayer nurtures our trust in God*. A good father would never neglect his children. And neither does your heavenly Father. As Jesus exclaimed when comparing earthly fathers to our heavenly Father, "how much *more* will your Father, who is in heaven, give good things to those who ask Him!" (Matthew 7:11). So we ask of Him, demonstrating our trust in Him. And then we demonstrate further trust in Him as we "look up" (Psalm 5:3) and wait for His answers and actions on our requests (James 5.16-18). As someone has quipped, "When the outlook is bad, try the uplook!" That "uplook" nurtures our trust in God.

And, too, *prayer guides us in the path of righteousness.* We've already discussed the necessity of praying before we read God's Word. Why? Because we so desperately need a soft, pliable heart so as not to miss God's message to us as we read. And there are other reasons we must pray for God's direction. For instance, because we so desperately desire to live in obedience. Because we so desperately want God's leading as we make decisions, both large and small, ranging from our service to God to the schedule we make for our busy day. Because we so desperately require God's help in order to live our lives His way. Because looking to God helps us to love others. Because our hearts are so desperately wicked (Jeremiah 17:9)! Through prayer we open up our hearts to God. And when we do, He searches them, ferrets out our motives, and affords us the opportunity to bring our wills into line with His plan.

In addition, *prayer assists our relationship with God.* The daily discipline and act of prayer helps maintain our relationship with God. And, when we fail, it also restores it.

—David confessed his transgressions unto the Lord...and then enjoyed the forgiveness of his sin (Psalm 32:5).

37

—David also cried out to God to have mercy upon him…and then experienced the restoration of the joy of his salvation (Psalm 51:1,12).

—Samson, too, in spite of past failure, beseeched God to "remember" him and to "strengthen" him for one more feat of power on God's behalf. The result? God used Samson one last time…to obliterate a pagan temple and its evil worshipers (Judges 16:23-31).

Another reason for praying is that *prayer strengthens us against our tendency to sin*. What does the Bible say to do instead of giving in to fretting, worrying, and anxiety? Pray (Philippians 4:6-7)! What does the Bible say to do instead of carrying grudges or succumbing to bitterness? Pray (Mark 11:25)! What does the Bible say to do instead of hating those who hurt us? Pray (Matthew 5:44)! When you are tempted to sin, pray, dear one, instead.

How Then Should We Pray?

Acknowledging that we *want* to pray and knowing that we *need* to pray, then…*how* should we pray? A handful of guidelines and disciplines from the Bible help us get started on the how-to's of praying.

✓ We should pray regularly. Jesus didn't say, "*If* you pray." He said, "*When* you pray" (Matthew 6:5-7). Our Lord assumed that prayer would be the habit of our lives…as it was for Him. He assumed that we would yearn to communicate with our Father…as He did. He assumed that drawing upon God for spiritual strength would be as needful and as natural for us as breathing and taking in air is for sustaining physical life. As another nineteenth-century saint, Bishop J. C. Ryle, put it, "Prayer is the very life-breath of true Christianity."[1]

✓ We should pray respectfully. God is our *heavenly Father*. Therefore He is not like us (Isaiah 55:8-9)! And He is not "the man upstairs," "the force," "the Big Guy," a part of "the powers that be," or "God as we know Him." No, God is holy, the King of glory, the Judge of all, the God of heaven and earth and of all the hosts, the Mighty God, and the Lord of Lords (to name just a few of His titles)! Therefore, we pray respectfully, approaching God with an element of awe.

✓ We should pray humbly. The Pharisees of Jesus' day prayed loudly...and "longly"! By contrast we as women with a passion for prayer are to pray with humility and sincerity, like the tax collector in Jesus' parable, who, standing afar off, would not so much as raise his eyes to heaven, but beat his breast, saying, "God be merciful to me a sinner!" (Luke 18:13). Beloved, this humble man was praised by our Lord.

✓ We should pray boldly. Does this sound contradictory to what I just said? Yes, we are humble, penitent sinners. But because of God's grace we humble sinners can approach the throne of His grace boldly and with courage so that we may receive His mercy and find His grace to help us in the time of our need (Hebrews 4:16).

✓ We should pray broadly. Just think of all the loved ones and people and concerns you have for so many at home and around the world. What a privilege to pray for them! And I just thought of another "just think"—just think of all the decisions you have to make, all the planning you must do, all the managing of your busy life for God that you must attempt! *Oh, how we need His help! And we can pray broadly about it all.*

✓ We should (and can) learn to pray…or at least to pray better! Jesus' own disciples were at a complete loss…until they asked the Master of prayer to teach them how (Luke 11:1).

Getting Down to the Disciplines

I'm in the process of reading a book titled *Ten Questions to Diagnose Your Spiritual Health*. One of the ten questions the writer of this book suggests we ask ourselves is, "Are the spiritual disciplines increasingly important to me?" I'm sure you're wondering, as I did, "Well, exactly what are the spiritual disciplines?" Author Donald S. Whitney answers our question this way—

> The spiritual disciplines are the God-ordained means by which we bring ourselves before God, experience Him, and are changed into Christlikeness….These devotional and sanctifying practices…[include] the private reading of and meditating on Scripture, individual prayer, fasting, solitude, and the keeping of a spiritual journal.[2]

"Individual prayer." Did you catch it? So we must ask ourselves—"Is the spiritual discipline of individual prayer increasingly important?" Then let's consider what it takes to *develop* the discipline of prayer, especially in the busy day in and day out life you and I live. Let's deal with *how* we can nurture this God-ordained spiritual discipline by which, as Mr. Whitney says, "we bring ourselves before God, experience Him, and are changed into Christlikeness." (Now, that's life management God's way! And what a glorious desire, passion, and attainment that would be!)

1. *Make a commitment*—Like the development of all good things in our lives, becoming faithful in prayer requires a commitment. I know that for the first ten years of my life as a Christian, I flopped and flailed—and failed!—in this vital area of prayer. It wasn't until I made a written commitment—written in the form of a prayer to God—that I began to seriously put in the work, so to speak, that the spiritual discipline of prayer demands. These were simple words, but they communicated my heart's desire to God and defined my commitment—"Lord, I dedicate and purpose to spend the next ten years (Lord willing) developing a meaningful prayer life."[3]

2. *Realize that prayer is not optional*—No, prayer is commanded! Therefore it seems to me that you and I must purpose to pray daily. Decide that you will set aside some portion of time each day—alone—for prayer. That time can be five minutes, ten minutes, fifteen minutes, or more. I personally set my kitchen timer for the number of minutes I decide upon. Somehow that act and the sound of the timer's ticking settles me down to the business of praying, which often leads to praying far beyond the timer's ring. Don't worry about the length of time for now. Just dedicate however many minutes it takes to get you started down this

sacred path of prayer. We'll apply the same two principles to prayer we used for Bible reading time—

Something is better than nothing
and
Always aim for more.

Once you've determined the amount of time, settled down in a place (your prayer place), set a timer (if it helps), and actually gone about the task of prayer, I think you'll find that, as the sweet hymn bids us, you'll want to "linger a while with Jesus." You'll realize the many lovely blessings and rewards of your time spent in prayer. You'll discover that your dedicated time isn't enough, and you'll surprise yourself by lengthening it. And, if your time is up and you have to move on to the other duties of your day, that's okay. You did it! You met with the Lord in prayer! You followed through on your commitment to pray! You took a step toward weaving the discipline of prayer into the fabric of your busy life!

My friend, this is how a passion is born, tended, and takes flight—through the decisions we make, through the mechanics we employ, through the faithful follow-through on our commitments, through the diligence of just doing it. Our efforts somehow help to create the backdrop against which we can enjoy communion with the Almighty through prayer. Somehow the acts we tend to think of as *un*-spiritual bring about the *spiritual* reality we long for. It's a mystery to me…and it's hard to write about the "mechanics" of something as celestial as prayer. But please, do faithfully tend to the routine, to the setup, to the preparation, to the management(!)…so that the sentiments of your heart are fulfilled and a passion for prayer is kindled to a red-hot blaze.

3. *Refuse to miss a day*—Just like our efforts in reading our Bible, so we should seek to pray *daily*. Like any muscle, the "muscle" of prayer must be used regularly to grow stronger. To be the strong women of faith and prayer—and passion—we so long to be, we must seek to forge via daily prayer an unbroken chain that reaches its way toward heaven.

In our last chapter I mentioned my "Quiet Times Calendar." I use this chart to instill and encourage the discipline of daily Bible reading. But I also used it as a tool and a measuring stick and a visual aid to keep track of my faithfulness to my commitment to daily prayer. Whatever it takes, dear one, whether gimmicks or gadgets, charts or calendars, notebooks or journals, devise *something* to help you with the discipline of daily prayer!

4. *Study the prayers of the Bible*—The preserved-forever prayers in the Bible serve as our best tutors in prayer. Through these impassioned words of others you and I can learn how to better approach God with the many matters of our busy and complex life.

I remember one extraordinary year that taught me much about prayer. As I began on January 1 in Genesis 1 with a goal of reading through my Bible in a year, I kept the book *All the Prayers of the Bible*[4] next to me. Each day as I read my Bible, I also read the inspiring thoughts and comments and analyses written in that book on any prayers that occurred in my daily Bible reading. What a treasure!

Another good source for such a study is verse-by-verse commentaries written by Bible scholars. These teachers give an in-depth breakdown of the contents of the prayers of the Bible. Such an exercise is an invaluable help to you and me with our prayer life as these study aids give us insights into the particulars of *why* these Bible people prayed, *how* they prayed, *what* they prayed, and the *results* of their praying. And...good news! These added exercises take only a few extra minutes per day! Truly, some small endeavors reap massive...and mighty!...rewards.

5. *Study the prayers of the saints through the ages*—I think I must have an entire shelf of books on prayers written and prayed by others! I read them because they, too, teach me how to pray. One volume I (as a woman!) especially love is *The Prayers of Susanna Wesley*.[5] I appreciate two things about these prayers. First, Susanna Wesley had a passion for God *and* a passion for prayer. Her heart is wide open to us through her recorded prayers and meditations. And second is the fact that Susanna Wesley gave birth to 19 children! (Talk about *busy!*) Without domestic help—and without her husband's presence for much of the time—she cared for her babies (nine of whom died) and her lively brood, schooling them herself...and yet she still set aside daily time for prayer. When I think of this dear woman and her taxing circumstances, I can only surmise that...there goes every woman's list of excuses for not praying!

Just one more thing about collecting the prayers of others. All prayer efforts are not bliss! There are dry days when your heart is apathetic, when your mind won't focus, when your tongue is tied. Rather than give up on prayer on such a day (and give in to dullness of heart!), I prime the prayer pump by praying one or more of these uplifting prayers of others. Somehow the heartfelt, spiritual outpourings of another warms my heart, tunes—and turns—my mind upward, and loosens my tongue...until finally the words and the fervor behind them become mine.

Looking at Life

I am blessed to have had in the past a wonderful, godly, older woman who taught me one of the great lessons of living and managing the Christian life. She cautioned me, "Never major on the minors."

Never major on the minors. Precious reader, these five words revolutionized my life! They launched a complete spiritual makeover in my life that is continuing to this day. I still, these several decades later, evaluate my every decision and activity and minute by this wise standard—"Never major on the minors." They move me to hold each activity up to the Lord and ask in prayer, "Father, does this fit into Your plan for my life? Will this help me to be a better steward of the time and abilities You've given me to serve You? Does this contribute to my good and to the good of others? Is this worthy of my time?"

And now it's time to look at your life, dear one. What are the current raging passions of your heart? Evaluate your activities, the way you spend your God-given time. Such an exercise will reveal your passions. For instance, I know women who work at scrapbooking...*all night long!* It's an out-of-control passion! I know women, too, who stay up half the night reading. Why? Because their reading is a passion! I know women who stay up so late watching television that it jeopardizes their family and their home life. (And that goes for staying up late on the Internet, too!)

Beloved, these activities are "minors"! And these women are "majoring on the minors," something we must be ever so careful not to do.

In this book we're addressing—and dreaming of—a life that's lived with passion and purpose. We're attempting the better management of our lives so that we better live out God's plan for us. So I must ask you, from my heart to yours, what is your purpose in life? Is it growing in Christ so that you can better serve God? Is it realizing God's plan and purpose for your life? Is it nurturing the spiritual disciplines that better enable you to bring yourself before God so that you are changed into Christlikeness? And do you live in fear of majoring on any minors?

Oh, dear sister, I'm so glad a mature Christian woman of faith passed her advice on to me…and now I'm passing it on to you—never major on the minors. Such a discipline will keep you and me from wasting our priceless and oh-so-costly, God-given time and life on secondary (and lower and lesser!) activities. *Then* we will have all of the time in the world to cultivate the spiritual disciplines in our needy life. *Then* we will have ample time for reading and studying God's precious and holy and life-changing Word! *Then* there will be no busy hindrances to choke out the time we need to experience God through the discipline of prayer. (Now, *these* are passions and pursuits truly worthy of staying up all night for!)

So, do you have time for prayer? Is prayer one of the developing passions of your life? It can be, you know, if you refuse to major on the minors when it comes to managing your life and choosing how you spend your time each day. Make these prayers of Susanna Wesley the passion of your own heart—

> In the morning, pray that "Every work I do below, I do it to the Lord."
>
> In the evening, pray "I give Thee praise, O God, for a well-spent day."[6]

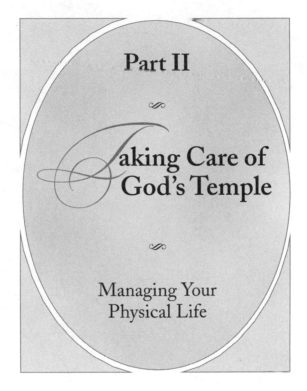

Part II

Taking Care of
God's Temple

Managing Your
Physical Life

Chapter 4

God's Guidelines
for Your Body

Your body is the temple of the Holy Spirit.
—1 CORINTHIANS 6:19

"Oh dear! I knew it was coming! And here it is—the physical area of life!"

Is this the kind of thought you're thinking as you look at the heading of this next section of our book? Well, you're not alone. I'm thinking and feeling the same way too! In fact, as the writer of this book, I've even thought of plenty of reasons for skipping the subject of the physical aspect of life altogether. Why? Because physical discipline is many times the most difficult to develop. It's a constant struggle. It's so often an area of sure failure for us as busy women. It's a realm requiring constant maintenance. Plus it's an unpopular topic and an area where people's opinions vary. There's no doubt it's a sore subject for many!

Yet there's also no doubt that gaining mastery over the body is an important part of every woman's life. And, I have to admit, it's grown into a vital one for me. Why?

First of all, because of *my Lord*. There is much shared from the heart of God in the Bible about managing the physical part of life. I finally came to the point in my spiritual growth that I concluded, "If my physical life is important to God, then it should be important to me!"

Next, because of *my family*. Just how do all those good housekeeping chores get done? How is a smooth-running, God-honoring household built and maintained? How is a lifetime of meals planned, shopped for, prepared, and lovingly placed on an eye-appealing table two to three times a day? How are affectionate relationships nurtured and developed? How does everyone in a family (including extended family) get prayed for, cared for, car-pooled, loved, and tended to? How does all the giving that God asks of His women get given? The answer somehow seems to boil down to energy—not only spiritual energy (as we learned from our previous chapters) but also *physical* energy.

Then there is the whole realm of *my ministry* to others in the body of Christ. God has gifted us as Christians to minister...and He expects us to do so by the use of our service and our spiritual gifts (1 Corinthians 12 and Romans 12). So...add ministry and service in the church to God's other assignments to us, and you and I can begin to topple if we don't take care of the physical sphere of our life!

What is the answer for us as busy women? Well, you and I both know that *God* is the answer. And God *has* the answers. And He's placed His answers and the all-important how-to's right in His Word. Therefore it's time to discover what God has to say to us as His women in the area of the physical. Let's discover the directions He gives us. After all, we want to do and be what He wants us to do and be!

1. Your body is a temple.

It was said by Dwight L. Moody, preacher of old and founder of the famed Moody Memorial Church and Bible Institute, that the secret to discipline is motivation, that when a person is sufficiently motivated, discipline will take care of itself.

Well, here's a concept that should provide the motivation for us as Christian women—your body is a temple. And not just any temple! As Paul exclaimed to the Corinthians who were involved in immorality, "Do you not know that your body is the temple of the Holy Spirit, who is in you, whom you have from God, and you are not your own?" (1 Corinthians 6:19).

As Christians in whose heart and body Jesus Christ dwells, you and I are temples of the Holy Spirit (1 Corinthians 3:16). Paul's reference to the Christian as a temple was made to the Corinthians because in his day the temple of the goddess Aphrodite was in Corinth. More than a thousand prostitutes helped to make sex a part of worship in the temple of Aphrodite.

Therefore, because the Spirit occupies that which is His own, Christians were—and are—to have nothing to do with sexual sin, no matter how popular or prevalent it is in the culture of the day.

So what does this mean to you and me as today's Christian women? What difference should it make to us that we house the Holy Spirit in our bodies? That our bodies are temples of God? Here's a little checklist that will help us to take better care of God's temples and our bodies.

> ✓ *Guard yourself*—All that you do, see, hear, think, eat, and choose must be guarded diligently. To keep the

temple of the Holy Spirit holy we must adhere to the wisdom of Proverbs 4. As we walk down through a portion of Proverbs 4, don't fail to note the intensity of the verbs, all of which are preceded by the understood subject "you."

> *Keep* your heart with all diligence, for out of it
>   spring the issues of life.
> *Let* your eyes look straight ahead,
>   and your eyelids look right before you.
> *Ponder* the path of your feet, and
> *Let* all your ways be established.
> *Do* not turn to the right or the left;
> *Remove* your foot from evil (verses 23-27).

✓ *Walk in righteousness*—And how does a righteous walk begin? By avoiding all temptations to even the *beginnings* of evil and unrighteousness! Proverbs 4 gives us a few more instructions on this worthy walk. In fact, we could well title it "How to Walk in Righteousness." And again, note the urgency of the staccato commands!

> Do not enter the path of the wicked. And
> Do not walk in the way of evil.
> Avoid it,
> Do not travel on it;
> Turn away from it, and
> Pass on (verses 14-15).

✓ *Avoid sexual sin* (1 Corinthians 6:13)—Never underestimate the power...and the destructiveness... of sexual sin! It has felled numerous giants of the faith, ruined countless lives, and devastated many a marriage and family. As God's child you are a member of Christ and joined to the Lord (verses 15 and 17). Therefore, sexual sin profanes our Lord Jesus Christ. Instead...

✓ *Fill your "temple"* with the beauty of holiness (Psalm 29:2)—As another preacher of old wrote, "Holiness is the architectural plan upon which God builds up His living temple."[1] The beauty of holiness was deemed by Jonathan Edwards to be "the greatest and most important thing in the world...for there is no other true excellence or beauty."

Dear one, when others look upon your life and lifestyle, do they see the beauty of holiness? Do they observe the behavior of a true godly woman who is "reverent in behavior" (Titus 2:3)? And, as you search your own mind and heart, are there perhaps some attitudes and practices you need to "put off" and "put away"? The New Testament calls us to "put to death" fornication, uncleanness, passion, and evil desire (Colossians 3:5). One gentleman made this decision regarding his "temple"—

> There are many activities I must cut out simply because I desire to excel in my pursuit after God and holiness.[2]

2. **Your body is not your own.**

We erroneously think we can do whatever we want with our bodies. After all, we mistakenly conclude, our bodies are our *own!*

But the truth is that God owns our bodies and that they are not ours. Paul's words shout to us across the centuries, with sort of an astounded and stinging "What?" He incredulously asks, "Do you not know that your body is the temple of the Holy Spirit who is in you, whom you have from God, and *you are not your own?*" (1 Corinthians 6:19).

As Paul explains it, "Now the body is...for the Lord" (verse 13). This means that as believers our bodies have been designed by God for *Himself* and for *His* purposes, not ours. The body of a believer is to be the instrument of the Lord. And it is to be used for *Him* and for *His* glory (verse 20).

Therefore, dear one, you and I are called by God and expected by God—and commanded by God—to live according to His rules and in such a way that brings glory to Him.

Let me explain it this way. Did you ever live in a dormitory? Or share an apartment with other women? Or stay in a camp facility? In these settings you more than likely helped to create or were issued a set of house rules. Why, even at home your parents probably had house rules.

Well, it's the same for you and me as Christians. Since your body belongs to God and is a house, a temple that houses the Holy Spirit, you are to live by God's rules, by the Owner's rules. You are not to violate the rules set by the Owner of the house or the temple.

And what are some of God's house rules? What are some of His rules for governing our bodies, which house the Holy Spirit and are the temples of God? To start off God's list, here is a short list of house rules for your body (which is, as we've learned, *His* body!).

- Flee sexual immorality (1 Corinthians 6:18).
- Flee also youthful lusts (2 Timothy 2:22).
- Do not love the world...
- ...or the things in the world (1 John 2:15).

- Abstain from fleshly lusts (1 Peter 2:11).
- Abstain from every form of evil (1 Thessalonians 5:22).

I trust you are getting the picture!

I imagine, too, that you are wondering why your body is not your own, why it belongs to the Lord. Well, here's God's answer—

3. Your body is bought with a price.

The Holy Spirit occupies only that which is His own. And, beloved, God has obtained your body at tremendous cost! He has purchased you to be His own. Your body has been bought with a price...and Jesus Christ paid the price to purchase you to be His own (1 Corinthians 6:20).

And how was that price paid? It was with the precious blood of Christ (1 Peter 1:18-19). Therefore, precious sister, you and I as Christians are not our own. No, we are *His* own (1 Corinthians 6:20 and John 13:1). Therefore, as one has pointed out, your body has been "purchased by Christ and is sanctified by the presence of God himself through his Holy Spirit. We must therefore sanctify it as well...by living the life of the Spirit, a life of holiness."[3] Therefore...

4. You are to glorify God in your body.

Our chief aim in life is to honor God. And, dear reader, that's what this book is about—managing our lives for the glory of God. And surely at the heart of every woman who desires to live out God's plan for her life with passion and purpose is a passion for glorifying God. Indeed, we are called to glorify God in all of life—"whether you eat or drink, or whatever you do, do all to the glory of God" (1 Corinthians 10:31), and specifically—to "glorify God in your body" (1 Corinthians 6:20). There's no doubt the body is a most significant part of our lives and needs to be managed to the glory of God. When we manage our bodies properly—God's way, that is—we give God honor. And, by the way, honoring God is a great motivator when it comes to mastering the disciplines needed in the physical area.

It's sobering to realize these few truths about the physical area of life—that our bodies are not our own but have been bought with a price, and that our bodies are the temples of the Holy Spirit and can (and should) be used in a way that glorifies God. That means that every act of sin you and I as believers commit in our very own bodies is being committed in God's sanctuary, His temple! Maybe we need to do as Robert Munger suggests—he is the creator of the timeless classic allegory "My Heart, Christ's Home"[4]—and go through our "temple," room by room, and clean it up (and out!) so that the beauty of holiness is indeed present and obvious. What are those rooms?

—The study. Are there any reading materials in your library that Christ's eyes are too pure to look upon? Why not replace them with the books of the Bible? Pack your bookshelves full of the Word of God and full of books about the Word of God!

—The dining room. This, explains Munger, is the room of appetites and desires. Are you feeding on fare fit for a child of the King? Food that feeds your soul and satisfies your spiritual hunger? What provisions are there that shouldn't be…and what nourishment needs to be there that isn't?

—The living room. According to this delightful story, the living room is where we are meant to meet morning by morning for quiet times filled with fellowship with Christ. Are you neglecting to enter this room as often as you should?

—The workroom. As the author has Jesus ask, "What are you producing with your life for the kingdom of God?" Toys? Gadgets? Are you whiling away the time God gives you working on hobbies? Or are you steadily going about the business of producing a masterpiece of your life for the glory of God? After all, you are His workmanship (Ephesians 2:10)!

—The rec room. What comprises your recreation and activities? With whom do you recreate? And what do you watch and listen to? Could Christ be a part of your "fun"?

—The bedroom. Here Christ speaks to the single reader about premarital sex and about relationships with the opposite sex. If you are unmarried, are you keeping yourself "holy in body and in spirit" (1 Corinthians 7:34)? And if you are married, are you careful in your purity with other men and your faithfulness to your mate?

—The hall closet. Cleverly, the author finally has Christ asking for access to a little locked-away place that contains a few leftover dregs of the old life that are personal favorites and have yet to be put away. I pray there is nothing in your life that needs to be tucked and hidden away in such a room in your "house"!

Does making your heart and body Christ's home sound too hard, too difficult? Does seeking to fill your "temple" with the beauty of holiness seem utterly impossible? Both you and I as God's women "must never allow ourselves to be mastered by anything or anyone—other than Jesus."[5] By God's great grace and able help, we can present Him a body that is dedicated to Him, ready (and fit!) to serve Him, seeking to honor Him, a living sacrifice (Romans 12:1).

Looking at Life

Well, dear patient one, we made it through several of God's guidelines for the body. There are more, but these few are the most powerful for motivating me in this area of the physical life! If we could simply live in light of our bodies being temples of the Holy Spirit, our daily life would be bettered, marked, changed, and transformed. Remembering this *one* truth at the waking end of each day—that our bodies are temples of the Holy Spirit—will most certainly fill the busy days of our lives with a greater passion for our worthy Lord. And then, if we add the fact that we are not our own, but are bought with a price, we can't help but eagerly desire to live out our obligation to faithfully serve our Master all the busy minutes of our lives for all the busy days of our lives!

Therefore, dear one, we should be about the business of "sanctifying" the Lord God in our bodies and in our hearts (1 Peter 3:15). To do this means we are to revere Christ as Lord and to hold Him in highest reverence. We are also to be consecrated, set apart, and dedicated to the Lord. And we are to honor Him with every facet of our lives—including our bodies. As Paul concluded, you and I are to "glorify God in your body and in your spirit, which are God's" (1 Corinthians 6:20).

Now, precious sister, do you yet sense the reverence? The respect? The awe? The magnitude of your body being *God's*? I pray so…and I also pray that with that realization comes a readiness to take the next step and live out that truth with a personal set of disciplines. So let's move forward. In the words of writer and lecturer Elisabeth Elliot,

~ *Discipline, for a Christian, begins with the body.* ~

Chapter 5

Ten Disciplines for Managing Your Body

Part 1

...glorify God in your body...
—1 CORINTHIANS 6:20

My son-in-law, Paul—the Paul married to my daughter Courtney—is a Navy submariner. That means he is routinely deployed for three months at a time. (Imagine being without your husband for 90 days...and with three preschoolers!) Anyway, during Paul's last deployment Courtney joined Weight Watchers to shed the predictable pounds that seem to accumulate after three babies (who, by the way are the cutest and smartest babies in all of Washington!).

What a joy it is for Jim and me to babysit one evening each week so Courtney can attend her Weight Watchers meeting and "weigh in." That means each week we are the first to hear as Courtney excitedly shares the good news of her weekly weight loss.

But each week Jim and I have also noticed an impressive change in other areas of Courtney's life—her attitude, energy level, and productivity are going up markedly as her weight is going down. This one discipline of watching what she eats has created an explosion of other disciplines in our Courtney's life. (And don't get me wrong! Courtney is already a wonderful and disciplined wife, mother, home-maker, and manager.) But Courtney agrees that with increased discipline in this one area of life she's been ener-gized in other areas as well.

The same is true for you and me, too, dear reading friend. We may not admit it (or want to admit it!), but the man-agement of our physical life has a domino effect on all the areas of our life. So let's look at some of the disciplines for managing the body that can reap a better attitude, greater energy, and increased productivity for us as busy women who desire to live out God's plan for our life…and who *must* live it out!

1. Pray for a healthy body.

Managing your life for God is a spiritual work, respon-sibility, and stewardship. And because our lives include physical bodies, those bodies must be managed. Therefore, the body's management falls into the spiritual realm, meaning you and I must pray earnestly and consistently about our bodies. Like the apostle Paul, we must pray not to be disqualified spiritually by an out-of-control body (1 Co-rinthians 9:27).

Are you trying to shed a few pounds? Then pray about the 20-plus food encounters statisticians tell us we face every day!

Are you trying to do a little exercising? Then pray to remain strong in spirit when your workout hour arrives… and you are sooooo tired!

Are you learning to make better food choices? Then pray (*before* you "fall" on your food—like the sinful Israelites did!)

to follow through on what you know will make you feel better, live better, and be a better servant to God and others.

Are you trying to break a bad habit—like staying up too late at night (which for most women leads naturally to munching and snacking after they've eaten dinner!)? Then pray to at least get yourself into your pj's and into your bed at an earlier hour. (That's half the battle. And don't forget to brush your teeth early, too! That's an almost-sure deterrent to further snacking.)

Are you battling a disease? Then pray, first of all, that God's strength will be perfected and manifest through your weakness (2 Corinthians 12:9-10). Then pray to God to lead you to the right physicians, physical therapists, nutritionists, medications, and books that will help you wage a better battle. Also pray to God to provide the people you'll need to come alongside you and cheer you up as well as physically assist you.

I could go on and on with everyday real-life scenarios, but it's obvious that prayer is one mighty spiritual weapon we can wield to manage our lives so that God is glorified. By now I hope you understand that whether you are getting up early to meet with the Lord, taking care of your family, working on the job, or serving in a ministry, health, energy, and stamina are required.

Personally, I've been on a lifelong quest for health, energy, and stamina since I was 33 years old. That's when I realized (thanks to my mirror!) that the days of my youth had indeed passed, that gravity was proving its powerful pull, and that the strength and endurance that had once come easily was beginning to shrivel away. That's when I began to pray for a healthy body. And with my devotion to pray about it came more vigilance, more discipline, more determination, and more dedication. The more I prayed and sought the Lord's wisdom and help, the more aware I became of God's plan for my life in the physical area. And the more I prayed, the more I tasted the many wonderful benefits that come from watching over body and health.

Our spiritual lives radically affect our physical lives. That's why I've placed the management of the physical area of life on the heels of the spiritual. And I think 3 John 2 bears this out. This verse is often misused and misconstrued. The apostle John is writing to his "beloved Gaius" to commend him for his generous hospitality and continued faith. Hear John's greeting—"Beloved, I pray that you may prosper in all things and be in health, just as your soul prospers."

Now hear scholar John MacArthur's comments on the apostle John's greeting, which highlights Gaius' vibrant spiritual condition: "Gaius' spiritual state was so excellent that John prayed that his physical health would match his spiritual vigor."[1]

Beloved, *I*, Elizabeth George, pray that *you* may prosper in all things and be in health, just as your soul prospers!

2. Acknowledge sin.

At first glance, we may not think this is an important discipline...but is it ever! The Bible is laced with examples of the physical body being affected by the spiritual condition. Listen as David gives a vivid testimonial of what happened to his body when he failed to acknowledge his sin.

> When I kept silent, my bones grew old
> through my groaning all the day long.

> For day and night Your hand was heavy
>   upon me;
> my vitality was turned into the drought of
>   summer (Psalm 32:3-4).

Now notice David's willful decision to confess his sin.

> I acknowledged my sin to You,
> and my iniquity I have not hidden.
> I said, "I will confess my transgressions to
>   the LORD,"
> and You forgave the iniquity of my sin
>   (verse 5).

And the result? Note the change in David's heart...and language!

> Be glad in the LORD and rejoice, you
>   righteous;
> and shout for joy, all you upright in heart!
>   (verse 11).

We must never doubt for a second that our spiritual condition affects our physical life! By dealing with our sin, you and I gain a greater measure of the physical vitality and health that fuels the life and the plan God has in mind for each of us. A passion for God should translate into a passion for dealing with sin. And beware if that passion is waning! As Paul wrote of the Corinthians who were participating in the Lord's Supper "unworthily" and with unconfessed and unforsaken sin, "for this reason many are weak and sick among you, and many sleep [are dead]" (1 Corinthians 11:29-30). True, confession may be bad for the reputation... but it sure is good for the soul!

3. Walk by the Spirit.

I'm so glad you and I have help—*spiritual* help—when it comes to the physical area of our lives! We just can't do it on our own! The pull of sin and the flesh is simply too strong.

God's help is available to us as Christians when we do as the apostle Paul teaches and "walk in the Spirit." And what happens when we walk in the Spirit? Paul gives the answer—"you shall not fulfill the lusts of the flesh" (Galatians 5:16). Instead we are empowered by "the fruit of the Spirit...self-control" (verses 22-23). Self-control is a critical key to managing all of life, including the physical life. And God's supernatural self-control is available to us when we walk by the Spirit. When we heed God's guidelines, pursue obedience, and look to Him for strength and grace, He helps us in any situation to deal with every temptation. This includes all of life—what we eat and drink, do and think.

So, my friend, instead of having a passion for food, pleasure, laziness, self-indulgence, and the things of this world (1 John 2:15), let's seek to walk by the Spirit and have a passion for wanting what God wants for our lives more than what we want. We aren't meant to live as we please. We're not meant to have what we want. And we don't have the right to live our lives any way we choose. Why? Because, as we've been learning, we are not our own but are bought with a price. Therefore, as *God's* woman, we are meant to live a life of self-denial, self-restraint, and self-control so that *God's* plan for our life is realized.

And then the pleasure...oh the pleasure...that comes from living out God's will! There is no other fulfillment like that of being all God wants you to be!

4. Discipline your body.

Hear Paul again. He writes, "I discipline my body and bring it into subjection, lest, when I have preached to others, I myself should become disqualified" (1 Corinthians 9:27). What does this mean? Other translations speak of this "discipline" as keeping under the body, beating and bruising the body, and making it a slave.[2]

Sounds awful, doesn't it? But here's the scene—Paul pictured life as a battle and his body as an opponent, an enemy. Therefore Paul disciplined himself and trained himself. He sought to gain mastery over his body. He practiced self-denial like an athlete, refusing to allow himself to waste time or become lazy or sidetracked. He wanted to be in shape for the battle. In short, he fought vigorously to win the battle over his body so that he could win the greater battle of successfully serving God.

But, my reading friend, the secret to Paul's discipline was a goal—he wanted to please God. And he wanted to achieve that goal of pleasing God so badly that there was no price too great to pay. He wanted to live out God's plan for his life. He wanted to realize God's will for his life. He wanted to make the good, better, and best choices. He wanted to "win the race" and feared failure.

So how can we join with Paul's passion and begin to discipline our body too? We've already mentioned several sure-fire ways—pray to be disciplined, and walk by the Spirit in obedience. And here's another one—as Christian women we are called to be temperate. That means we are to live in moderation. We are to develop a take-it-or-leave-it attitude toward food, passions, possessions, and emotions. Nothing is to have control over us. Instead, we are to have control over everything. (And thanks be to God for providing the grace of His self-control!)

So we say *no*. Try it! The next time you want a large portion of some tempting food, or a second helping, say *no* to your body and pass it up. The next time you want to laze in bed after the alarm's gone off, say *no* to your body and get up. The next time you are working along on your schedule for your day—a schedule that you believe will help you to live out God's plan for your busy day—and a friend calls and says, "Hey, let's get together! Want to come over? Want to meet for lunch?" graciously say *no*, schedule a future time to meet, and stay on your plan.

To live out God's plan for your life calls for you to discipline yourself...and your body. To push yourself. To deny yourself. So...get *into* the race! Then *run* the race. Then run the race *to win!*

And remember these few things along the way—

✓ Christ did not say "fulfill yourself." He said "deny yourself" (Matthew 16:24).

✓ George Mueller once said, "I cannot take care of my soul, God can keep that; but my body is for me to take care of."[3]

✓ And, oh, yes...Paul did not say "buffet" your body (as in treating it to a smorgasbord!). Paul said "buffet" your body (as in beating it into subjection!).

5. **Exercise regularly.**

Believe it or not, this week the weather experts on the Weather Channel switched hats and became "physical fitness experts," sharing a few things about exercise and health.

The feature reporter passed on the fact that studies have proven that people who exercise even for a few minutes each day experience less illness.

This statement made me think of this particular point in our chapter on the disciplines for our bodies. It seemed to bear out Paul's advice to his young protégé, Timothy, that there is such a thing as healthy, practical piety, that "bodily exercise profits a little" (1 Timothy 4:8). Paul explained that while godliness is good for *all* things, bodily exercise does help and benefit us a *little* while we're on this earth. Training the body is good, useful, even essential, and it does have value. What are just a few of the benefits realized by just a little exercise?

You'll look better, feel better, and enjoy better health and heightened physical energy, which tends to heighten your emotional and mental energy. You'll have less weight to lug around, which translates to less trauma to your joints, a greater desire to participate in life, and more energy for serving and giving to others. And how about these two additional payoffs—you'll sleep better and, as the reporter shared, you'll be less prone to illness.

I shared in the previous chapter about my physical turning point at age 33. What did I do about the downhill slide my body was taking? I did the simplest of all exercises—I began walking. Somewhere I had read that if you walk 20 minutes a day four days a week, you will lose 12 pounds in a year...without even changing your eating habits! So I began walking. And friend, I'm still walking!

And it's a glorious time! If I'm outside when I walk, I have God's creation to behold. I've watched the seasons roll in and out, the vegetation change, the atmosphere alter. I've seen sunrises, sunsets, cloud formations that were too breathtaking to even describe. I've tasted the sun, the wind, the rain, the cold, and the heat. And my companions on my walks are my memory verses, which I memorize and review…which transform my physical exercise into a spiritual one! And if I'm walking inside on our treadmill, I have other treats. I have Bible teaching videos and tapes to keep me going…and growing in the Lord!

I hope you realize the importance of exercise. Paul has put in his recommendation…and so has the Weather Channel…and so have I! I hope you're sensing the value of regular exercise as a part of successful life management and physical well-being. Stamina and energy are needed to live out God's plan for our lives. And that stamina and energy are boosted by regular exercise.

Most of the women I meet agree that exercise is important. And they agree that they should make it a regular part of their days and their lives. But many fail to make it a reality. So ask yourself, is exercise really important to you? Then how will you fit it into your routine?

For my lifestyle I've determined that the best time to exercise is really the worst time—at the end of my long days. Every one of them is long, busy, full, even exhausting. And at the end, I'll admit, I'm tired! My first thought is to get into my pj's, turn on my electric blanket, and go to sleep! But, because physical discipline has become a lifestyle, I take that worst time of the day and make it my exercise time. And guess what? By the time I'm finished, I've renewed my energy and am motivated to do what I refer to in my book on the Proverbs 31 woman,[4] "a little night work." I know you're busy, but pick a time…even the worst time…and begin to exercise regularly. You'll feel better. Your family will benefit too. Plus you'll be more productive. And God will be honored as you live out His plan for your life with passion and purpose…and energy!

Looking at Life

Wow! As we look back at what we're learning about disciplining our physical lives, it's obvious how essential discipline is to living out God's plan for our lives. We've already covered five major practices we can fold into our life that will improve our service to God and others—prayer, dealing with sin, walking by the Spirit, and disciplining and exercising our body. And there are more!

But let's pause right now. Reread or scan through this chapter again. Think about what we're learning. Mark out the disciplines you want to go to work on. Then pray! Pray about your life. Pray about your body. Pray about your energy level. Pray about your attitude toward your life and your work. And pray about your productivity.

And then prepare your heart to discover in the next chapter five more ways to manage yourself and your body for greater godliness.

Chapter 6

Ten Disciplines for
Managing Your Body

Part 2

...glorify God in your body...
—1 CORINTHIANS 6:20

In the previous chapter I tried to share many of the wonderful benefits my daughter Courtney is reaping from paying attention to her physical life, and more specifically, to her eating habits. Yes, Courtney is greatly blessed by her efforts.

But, my friend, I have to pass on yet another blessing: Jim and I have been blessed too! How? Because we were so impressed by what we witnessed in Courtney's life that we were motivated and stimulated to do the same. We wanted what Courtney had. So we put on the skids, buckled down, rolled up our sleeves, and went to work on our eating habits. Now we too are reaping some of the benefits that she is enjoying. We too are experiencing the energy and attitude changes and productivity that are possible for everyone who manages their body God's way. (And who knows? Maybe our disciplines will affect someone else. And who knows? Maybe yours will too!)

Now let's look at five more disciplines for us to put into practice.

6. Seek proper sleep and rest.

"What's going on?" That's the question my doctor was asking me as I showed up in his office...again...complaining of a throat condition that was becoming chronic.

With his words echoing through my mind, I too began to ask, "What's going on?" Well, I went home and made a list, and here's what was going on at that season of my life—

Sunday	Church all morning (sing in the choir for two services) and church all evening
Monday	Prepare women's Bible class lecture all day and teach women's Bible class all evening
Tuesday	Prepare Bible study lecture all day (and all night!)
Wednesday	Teach women's Bible study lecture all morning and teach seminary wives class all evening
Thursday	Choir practice all evening

Once I made this list, I could clearly *see* what was going on. I simply wasn't getting enough rest and sleep. And my body was letting me know it! Something had to give. And it was the schedule...or me.

I knew what the Bible said about the need for rest and sleep. (I also knew what it said about laziness!) But as I thought through my situation, my mind went first to Jesus, who urged His busy and weary disciples to "come aside by yourselves to a deserted place and rest a while" (Mark 6:31).

74

Then I thought of God's busy and tired prophet Elijah. Stretched to the limit by the strain of intense ministry, by threats of peril, and by debilitating fatigue, Elijah collapsed. How tenderly God cared for His spent servant! First there was rest and glorious sleep...only to be interrupted by the touch of an angel who summoned Elijah to eat. Then there was another bout of sleep...and another angelic wake-up call to still another meal. And then the Bible says Elijah, after rest and food and drink, "went in the strength of that food forty days and forty nights" (1 Kings 19:1-8).

After much prayer and with Jim's guidance, I made some painstaking decisions about the hours of my days and nights. It was obvious my busy-ness scale had tilted and I was headed for a fall. The little quip was living itself out in my life—"When your output exceeds your input, then your upkeep will be your downfall!" As a result, I made some corrections in my lifestyle that allowed for proper rest and sleep.

Ask yourself "What's going on?" regarding the hours of your days (and nights!). Where on the need scale does your sleep and rest pattern fall? For most women it falls on one end or the other. Do you need a little more sleep and rest? Or are you getting a little too much as the proverb warns us— "A little sleep, a little slumber, a little folding of the hands to sleep—so shall your poverty come on you like a robber, and your need like an armed man" (Proverbs 6:10-11)? Now, what will you do to balance out any extreme?

7. Watch what you eat.

One year an "older" spiritually mature woman shared with me that she reads through her Bible every year looking for what the Bible says about one specific topic. Well, because of my great admiration for this woman's life (and

75

passion and purpose), I decided to follow her example (and have been doing so ever since). Anyway, on one of my reads through my Bible, I picked the subject "food" and marked out every reference to food and health and nutrition. I even noted the specific foods referred to and whether that reference was favorable or not. That exercise of paying attention to what the Bible says about food was quite revealing! For instance, I learned...

A lesson from Daniel—Daniel was one of God's people who was carried away from his homeland and family to be enslaved in Babylon (Daniel 1:1-21). Set apart for three years to be groomed to serve the king, Daniel and his three friends were appointed a daily provision of "the king's delicacies and of the wine which he drank" (verse 5). But Daniel "purposed in his heart" that he would not "defile" himself with the king's food and wine (verse 8). Instead he and his three fellow Israelites asked for vegetables and water (verse 12). Amazingly, after only ten days, all four young men looked "better and fatter in flesh" than all those who ate the king's rich foods (verse 15)! And when the three years of preparation and training were up, Daniel and his friends were brought before the king to be examined. The result? The king "found them ten times better than all the magicians and astrologers who were in all his realm" (verse 20).

Of Daniel's life, author and lecturer Elisabeth Elliot observes, "Discipline is evident on every page of the life of Daniel....The first thing that sets Daniel apart...is [a] decision [regarding] food....It was the beginning of the Lord's preparation of a man whose spiritual fiber would be rigorously tested later on."[1]

Taking a page out of Daniel's book, I've been trying to eat for health and energy. There is so much I want (and need!) to do to serve my husband and family. And I want to enjoy the blessings of a smooth-running home. Plus, there are the many things I want to do to serve the Lord. So, believe me, I pay attention to everything I eat, even *when* I eat it. After every meal or snack, I intentionally notice whether I feel heavy-headed and tired, or refreshed and energized. Then I make note of what I ate that either sapped my energy or supplied the next needed boost of strength.

A lesson from Jonathan—And make sure you do eat! That's a lesson we learn from the life of Jonathan, the son of King Saul (1 Samuel 14:24-31). Saul had issued a rash oath during a heated battle against the Philistines stating, "Cursed is the man who eats any food until evening, before I have taken vengeance on my enemies." And the result? "None of the people tasted food" even though they were "very faint" (verse 31).

Except Jonathan. Not knowing of His father's curse, Jonathan came with all the people to a forest where honey had dripped onto the ground. Tired from battle, Jonathan quite naturally dipped the tip of his spear into the honey and ate some of the nourishing, sweet liquid. The Bible reports that immediately "his countenance was brightened" (verse 27). God's lesson is summed up in the words of Jonathan, "How much better if the people had eaten freely today!" (verse 30).

Food is God's way of fueling your body with energy and health for the work you must do. Your car needs gas, doesn't it? Well, dear one, you do too! So, as I said, be sure you do eat. Just watch what you eat! As someone has noted, "the best exercise is to exercise discretion at the dining table."[3]

8. Keep a schedule.

Or put another way, develop a routine. One management expert teaches that a routine "makes unskilled people without judgment capable of doing what it took mere genius to do before."[3] What a statement! It's staggering to think that the simple and singular discipline of keeping a schedule could make us look—and perform—like geniuses! But it's true. A routine allows even the busiest of women to work at a steady pace without having to race through the day, and yet accomplish the majority of her many tasks.

Jesus and His schedule—Jesus certainly exemplifies this picture of a busy person in the midst of a busy life. Yet He never seemed to be in a hurry. He was never rushed and never breathless. He just continued moving purposefully through His schedule and His day. In fact, Jesus' routine was so predictable that Judas knew exactly where to find Him when he brought the mob to arrest the spotless Lamb of God (John 18:2).

You and your schedule—So, like our Lord, you must create a schedule and develop a routine. The reason Jesus was so unhurried in his schedule was that His schedule was based on God's priorities for His life. And, dear one, when our schedule reflects God's priorities for us as His women, then we will never be too busy to accomplish God's plan for our day...and for our life. So when I say make and keep a schedule, I mean this—determine God's priorities for your life and develop a schedule that is centered on those priorities.

Such a schedule will certainly simplify your life. You'll find yourself not having to think so much about every detail

78

of your day because you've scheduled in your priorities. You'll worry less about whether or not you're spending your precious time on the right endeavors. You'll seem to flow from one task and portion of your day to the next.

And don't forget to establish a routine that fits your particular stage of life and responsibilities. Then adjust your schedule as your life shifts from one stage to another. When you have children, one schedule is called for. As they grow up, there's another. Then there's the empty nest with its own unique need for routine and a schedule. Just start *where* you are today...and *start* today!

Are you unsure about what your schedule and routine should be? Then dare to take a look at the busy days of the woman described in Proverbs 31:10-31. Note when she got up, when she went to bed, and what she did in-between. (No wonder she is heralded by God as a woman who looked well to the ways of her household...and her life [verse 27]! Now there's a woman who lived out God's plan and God's priorities for her life with both passion *and* purpose!)

9. Take care of your appearance.

It's interesting that the Bible contains very little about the outward appearance of the physical body. Perhaps that's because the Bible is a spiritual book and focuses our attention on the "inner" man and woman (2 Corinthians 4:16). And the apostle Paul goes on to point out what we already know about the physical body (just look in the mirror...like I did at age 33!)—"our outer man is decaying."

But there are definite ways you and I can take care of our appearance so that the "outer" woman at least looks her best.

And God does comment on the outward appearance of some of the women of the Bible. For instance,

- Sarah was called a beautiful woman by her husband Abraham (Genesis 12:11).

- Both Rebekah and Rachel were described as beautiful of form and face (Genesis 24:16 and 29:17).

- The exquisite Esther took care of her appearance, dressed with care, and "obtained favor in the sight of all who saw her" (Esther 2:15).

- We don't know what the Proverbs 31 woman looked like, but we do know that her clothes were special—fine silk and purple (Proverbs 31:22).

It seems clear that beauty and the care of your appearance has a place in the arena of physical discipline. Don't worry so much about what you look like. You look exactly as God meant you to look, for, indeed, you are "fearfully and wonderfully made" (Psalm 139:14). But you can make an effort in the care of your appearance. So fix up...a little! Make up...a little! Dress up...a little! Shape up...a little! (Others will be most grateful!)

10. Commit to a lifelong pursuit of discipline.

Whenever I'm feeling especially worn out (or worn down!) or discouraged, I have several favorite verses that provide a sure pick-me-up. One is Paul's testimony about his lifelong pursuit of disciplined service to God and others—"I have fought the good fight, I have finished the race, I have kept the faith" (2 Timothy 4:7). And another is Paul's encouragement to the Corinthians (which always seems to be shot straight from God's heart to Paul's heart and right on through to mine!)—"Therefore, my beloved brethren, be steadfast, immovable, always abounding in the work of the Lord, knowing that your labor is not in vain in the Lord" (1 Corinthians 15:58).

Maybe it's because at one time I was an English teacher, but I pay careful attention to verbs, the part of each sentence that indicates action. And I can't help but notice that verbs like *strive, reach, press, endure, fight, run,* and *continue* are liberally sprinkled throughout the New Testament. All of these verbs and the verses they appear in point me to the fact that the Christian life and the management of my Christian life is not a sprint or a spurt or a sputter. My life is not to be characterized by false starts, fad diets, flashy gimmicks, or flashes of discipline followed by long periods of self-indulgence and/or neglect. No, the verbs in these verses encourage me to embrace the fact that life management is a "marathon" characterized by a long-sustained, steady pace of running that is required for running the disciplined race of a life of dedication and service to God.

Looking at Life

Jim and I had the once-in-a-lifetime privilege of being in one of the last audiences addressed by J. Oswald Sanders before his death. Dr. Sanders was a renowned missionary statesman and author of the classic book *Spiritual Leadership*.[4] This saint and Christian legend was in his nineties at the time we heard him. A little unsteady on his feet, he was helped up the six steps to the podium by several men. Finally, holding on to the pulpit with both hands, Dr. Sanders began his message. He started slowly...but soon all could sense and see the strength of God empowering him as he delivered a dynamic sermon to the several thousand people in the audience.

What we witnessed on that memorable evening was the end-product of a life spent developing the disciplines that kept a man in the Christian race and sustained his service to the end. Dr. Sanders had a message and a ministry—even in his sunset years—because of a lifetime of days spent reading God's Word. He was still reading, still sharp, still studying, and still growing in Christ as he drew nearer and nearer to meeting his Lord face to face. And he was "lean and mean" in appearance—not puffy, not perspiring, not breathless, not pasty—but exhibiting the fortitude and health that a life-time of physical discipline had built in and built up.

This is what I desire for you and me, my dear sister—that we, like J. Oswald Sanders, would discipline ourselves in the spiritual and physical areas so we can serve our Lord and our loved ones and God's people with strength and power to the very end of our busy life. That we will be clear-headed and possess the physical strength and stamina to strive and reach and press on each and every day toward the upward call of God in Christ Jesus (Philippians 3:14). To do this will require us to commit to a lifelong pursuit of discipline. In the words of writer John Maxwell, we must acknowledge that "self-discipline can't be a one-time event. It has to become a lifestyle."[5]

Part III

Creating a Heaven
on Earth

Managing Your
Home Life

If anyone is in Christ, he is a new creation;
old things have passed away;
behold, all things have become new.
—2 CORINTHIANS 5:17

I'm sure you've heard these three words before—*heaven on earth*. Exactly what comes to your mind when you hear them? If you're like me, you usually think of bliss, pleasure, peace, joy, perfection, and order.

But...did you know that your home life is meant to convey a picture of heaven on earth to others—and especially to your family members? That's right! In the Bible God uses marriage and home life as an illustration of His relationship with His church (Ephesians 5:22-25). And when family members live out their God-ordained roles and fulfill their God-given assignments, others witness the relationship God has with His people.

Heaven on Earth

Beloved, you and I have the privilege of presenting a picture to others of what heaven will be like. We have the opportunity to turn our homes into a little bit of heaven on earth. When we pursue God's design for us as wives, mothers, and homemakers and pursue it with passion and purpose, we establish a place here on earth that reflects the bliss and order of our future home in heaven.

Therefore, in this section of our book on life management for busy women, prepare yourself to look first into God's Word for His guidelines. Then we'll look straight into the Lord's eyes and set about to do what His Word says we must do. Also prepare yourself to purpose to set aside all meaningless and peripheral busy-ness and to spend the rest of your life paying whatever the cost—whether in time or in effort—to take good care of this most important priority of life. Your family life is important to God. Therefore it should (and must!) be important to you.

I wish I knew you better. More than that, I wish we could sit down and talk. I wish I knew the stage of life you are in. I wish I knew if you are married or not, if you have ever been married, if you have children, grandchildren, where you live, what your home atmosphere is like. But I don't. So I'll go ahead with these chapters, trusting God that these truths will help you in your closest relationships. I also pray that God's Word will help you to help other women to better manage their family life (Titus 2:3-5).

A Word of Testimony

I am married. And, I should quickly add, *by the grace of God* I'm still married! When Jim and I married 35-plus years ago, Jim was a Christian but I was not. That means we were unequally yoked. (And as the joke goes, "If a child of God marries a child of the devil, said child of God is sure to have some trouble with his father-in-law!" Believe me, we had our troubles!)

As you can see, we began our marriage at a disadvantage. And, I must add, we did everything wrong! In our marriage there was no leader…and no follower. There were few or no standards, and the ones we had were not God's standards. We had no rules to guide us.

Soon our messed-up-life-of-two became a messed-up-life-of-four as two little ones were added to the family. Our situation went from bad to worse as we now also lacked principles for raising our children.

And, oh, yes, I don't want to forget to tell you that I was off doing my own thing, pursuing my own dreams. With a husband, a home, and two preschoolers, I went back to school (in marriage and family counseling, of *all* things!). The hours in my days were spent dropping my children off every morning in the dark at a babysitter, attending classes as a full-time student, picking my little ones up from the babysitter after dark, and then immersing myself in the bookwork and paperwork required when pursuing an advanced degree. (Talk about busy!) No, our home was not a heaven on earth for any of us. No home will *ever* be a heaven on earth when the marriage, the family, or the home is neglected. And I was three for three! I was neglecting them all!

As I said at the beginning of this book, by God's grace, my soul was saved, my marriage was saved, my family was saved, and my home was saved. The reality of becoming a child of God was proven as 2 Corinthians 5:17 was realized in my life—"if anyone is in Christ, he is a *new* creation; old things have passed away; behold, all things have become *new*."

Suddenly, for the first time in my life, I had something— something *new*—to build my life on, something to pattern my life after, and that was the Word of God. And suddenly, for the first time in my life, I had something—something *new*—to empower my life, and that was the power of God working in my life through His Holy Spirit. Yes indeed, *I* was a new creation...and suddenly *all things* had become new!

So I dove into my Bible (after I purchased one, that is!). I devoured the words and the teachings of my Bible. I was like that newborn babe in 1 Peter 2:2 who desires the pure milk of the Word so that it can grow! I have to report that I didn't resist following much of what I read there in the Bible. No, I was desperate. I was dying...and so was my dream of a happy marriage and family life. And now I had answers—not man's answers, but *God's* answers.

I've shared at length in several of my other books about what I've learned from the Bible about marriage, family, and home done *God's* way.[1] So what I offer here in a book about managing all the urgent areas of your life are some of the key principles and guidelines on each of these three areas that wrap their arms around the teaching of God's Word to you and me as a wife, a mother, and a home-manager. It won't be exhaustive...but the basics are here.

Now, let's examine the basics for managing this all-important area of your family life. Let's see what it takes to create a little bit of heaven on earth.

Chapter 7

Managing Your Marriage

This is my beloved, and this is my friend.
—Song of Solomon 5:16

Falling in love is easy.

But *growing* a Christian marriage and *nurturing* a life-long friendship and *building* a permanent, rewarding relationship takes work—*hard* work! It takes commitment. It takes determination. It takes time and sacrifice. And it takes daily management.

Next to your relationship with God, your marriage is most urgent—and demanding! Yet the meticulous management of your marriage relationship pays many of life's highest dividends. I don't know about you, but whenever anything is wrong between my husband and me, I am miserable. I can enjoy great accomplishments on many fronts... but if something is wrong with my priority relationship with Jim, then all is wrong. Life seems soured.

If you are married and you want to live out God's plan, then as a wise woman you must make certain that you go above and beyond the call of duty when it comes to managing your marriage. God, who knows our needs, has provided His guidelines for our marriage in His Word.

God's Guidelines for Marriage

What is it God expects of you and me as wives? I've identified what I call "God's Four Words for Wives." They have been lifesavers (and marriage-savers) for me.

Help your husband—(Genesis 2:18). God declared, "It is not good that man should be alone; I will make him a *helper* comparable to him." And that helper is you, if you are married. That means you are to set aside self in order to make helping your husband a priority. That means you are to spend your days and your life helping and assisting your mate with his responsibilities and his stewardship of the family. There's no reason you shouldn't go to bed after each day spent helping your husband and imagine God's personal "Well done, dear Christian wife!" Such a day would be one lived out in a way that honors God and His Word. It would also be a day that benefited your husband. And such a day should be repeated daily as long as you have a husband.

Follow your husband's leadership—(Ephesians 5:22). This principle represents God's will for every married woman. We may not understand this guideline. We may not perceive how in the world it will work or why God would ask it of us. We may not like it. And we may think that in our modern do-your-own-thing, I-am-woman world, God's guideline of submitting to our husbands is outdated and prehistoric, even barbaric. But read Ephesians 5:22-24 for yourself. Mark it. Underline it. Highlight it. Memorize it.

It's there, precious one, written from God's heart to ours... for our good and for His glory! It's a part of His divine recipe for a happy, fulfilling marriage.

Respect your husband—(Ephesians 5:33). What are some ways we demonstrate that we respect our husband? There are many little ways. For starters, *look at him.* Just stop, and physically turn your gaze upon your husband whenever he speaks. *Never talk about him.* If you have a problem, see your pastor or a counselor in your church. But all others must only hear your lips blessing your husband. *Ask him.* When you're asked to do something or make a decision, always say, "I'll have to check with my husband first." (As I said, these are "little" things...but they say a lot!)

Love your husband—(Titus 2:4). Our first duty as wives is to make our home life attractive and beautiful by loving our husbands. (Remember...heaven on earth!) "Love is the highest blessing in an earthly home, and of this the wife...is the natural center."[1] So roll up your sleeves and get busy loving your husband. Nurture your love for him. Show him your love. Lavish him with your love! Show him the kind of attention you would show to a best friend. After all, your heart and affection should echo that of the Shunammite's emotion toward her husband Solomon, when she declared, "This is my beloved, and this is my friend" (Song of Solomon 5:16). Your loyal love will work wonders in your marriage. So...

> When he is sad, cheer him.
> When he is noble, praise him.
> When he is generous, appreciate him.
> When he is talkative, listen to him.
> When he comes or goes, kiss him.[2]

These four guidelines—help him, follow him, respect him, love him—can and should translate into four lifetime goals for you if you are married. And these next ten disciplines should assist you in the management of your marriage.

Ten Disciplines for a Meaningful Marriage

1. You shall center your life on the Lord.

God declares that, as a basis for godly family relationships, His Word is to first "be in *your* heart" (Deuteronomy 6:6). Proverbs 4:23 also warns, "Keep *your* heart with all diligence, for out of it spring the issues of life."

Dear wife, don't worry about what your *husband* is or isn't doing to cultivate his spiritual life. Concern yourself with making sure *you* are a godly *wife*, that *your* life is centered on the Lord. Then *you* will be a vessel God can work through. And even if there are no changes in your husband or in the tone of your marriage, *you* will walk through each day with God's wisdom and grace, with God's strength and dignity (Proverbs 31:25). *You* will be conformed to the image of your dear Savior (Romans 8:29)...and God will be glorified by *your* behavior (Titus 2:5). No woman can ever live a more meaningful life than that of developing, in Christ, the character qualities that mark a life (and a wife) focused on God.

2. You shall pray for your husband.

Here's another discipline that requires us to set aside more of our busy-ness. (And that's exactly what it will require for us to become women and wives of prayer!) Through prayer, refresh your commitment to your marriage and your husband daily. You'll find an amazing thing happening as you spend your precious time praying for your husband and your marriage. You'll find Christ's principle to be true of you—"Where your treasure is [i.e., the treasure of your time and earnest spiritual effort spent in prayer], there your heart will be also [i.e., your heart will become consumed with the object of the treasure of your time and prayers—your husband!]" (Matthew 6:21). Prayer changes things—things like a wife's heart and a marriage.

3. You shall know your roles.

Remember "God's Four Words for Wives"—help him, follow him, respect him, and love him. It wouldn't hurt to include in your prayer time each day a fresh commitment to live by these four guidelines. These roles should become part of your thought process and actions each day.

4. *You shall study your mate.*

> When you marry him, love him.
> After you marry him, study him.[3]

Are you a student of your husband? For instance, what are his likes and dislikes? This area of knowing and honoring your husband's likes and dislikes is yet another area where you can demonstrate your respect for him (Ephesians 5:33). Are you aware of his moods, his timetable, when he likes to talk and when he doesn't, his work schedule, his energy cycles? Have you figured out the best time to approach him about the important matters of life and the best way to speak to him? Do you know what's going on at his workplace? Do you know if any pressures are building up

93

in his life? Your husband is the most important person in your life. Therefore, you should know him—inside and out!

5. You shall be a servant.

Marriage is more than *finding* the right person. It is *being* the right person! Think not of yourself...but of your mate. From your waking moment to lights-out, set about to serve your husband in as many ways as possible. Remember, your role is to be his helper (Genesis 2:18). It's nice if he helps you once in a while, but don't get caught up in expecting it...or resenting it when it doesn't happen! Look instead to Christ's example, for Jesus came, not to *be* served, but *to* serve (Matthew 20:28).

6. You shall follow your husband's leadership.

We've already mentioned God's guideline of the husband as the head in the marriage (Ephesians 5:23). His role of leader in the marriage doesn't mean you can't learn how to communicate openly, honestly, and sweetly with your husband, presenting your case, even appealing. But it does mean that you go into each situation with the mindset that you are going to follow your husband's leadership if at all possible. I've learned that many times I, as a wife, have to do what God is asking *me* to do—submit—so that *He* can work in my husband's life. And many times God ultimately works in my life...as I see *after* my step of faith, *after* my submission, that my husband's direction was best!

I know it's hard, but ask God to help you take some small initial steps in submission. Test the water, trust the Lord, and defer to your husband's leadership. It can be as small as quietly going to *his* choice of restaurant...instead of whining, objecting, demanding, or just plain ol' having "a better idea" regarding where the two of you should eat!

7.   You shall make sure your husband is #1.

Even before there was such a thing as a parent, God laid down this principle for a healthy marriage—"a man shall leave his father and mother" (Genesis 2:24). Jesus repeated this principle (Mark 10:7-8), and so did Paul (Ephesians 5:31). For the best marriage possible, both husband and wife are to *leave* (the union and the emotion previously enjoyed with parents and family) and to *cleave* (glue themselves to their mate). Simply stated, we are to place our husband first in our life, in our heart, and in our time. Our husband is to be a higher priority than our children, parents, family, friends, Christian women, work and workmates, hobbies, etc. Our husband is to be second only to God in our allegiance and loyalty.

Let's face it—as busy women we have *a lot* of people and activities in our life! But God is clear when He says we are to leave our families (and everything else) and cleave to our husbands. We are to make sure he's #1!

8.   You shall talk things over.

Learn to talk things over with your husband. This will require a commitment, first of all, to listen to him. Plus you'll have to ask lots of questions. It's important that you and your husband seek to agree on the many issues that challenge any marriage—finances, raising the children, the daily schedule, your priorities and goals as a couple, how you spend your evenings and weekends... and vacations (this one can get very sticky!).

Just remember that communication is the goal—not arguing, not emoting, not winning. So be sure you practice another of God's good-communication-in-marriage rules— "Do not let the sun go down on your wrath" (Ephesians 4:26). In other words, don't go to bed angry. Talk things over instead.

9.   You shall heed a few "don'ts."

Don't be contentious (Proverbs 19:13; 27:15). *Don't* nag like the constant drip that drives one insane (Proverbs 27:15). And *don't* embarrass your husband by your speech, your appearance, your behavior, or your neglect of family and home (Proverbs 31:11-12).

10.   You shall make each day fun.

Do you remember how much fun you and your sweetie had when you were dating? The crazy things you did? The laughter? The fun? Well, step back into those "happy days" and make sure each day involves the same light-hearted joy. After all, a husband and wife are to continually rejoice in one another (Proverbs 5:18). Hopefully, you and/or your relationship are not too far gone that you have to think too long and hard to follow this cheerful commandment!

Did you run across any assignments here that God cannot help you to follow through on? Of course not! So let's begin now to put them to work!

Dear one, for as long as God allows you to enjoy marriage, live out His principles so that you *and* your precious husband will be abundantly blessed!

Looking at Life

Here's a question to ponder. Are you too busy to manage your marriage God's way? Perhaps one reason you're too busy is because all of your busy-ness eases the pain of a too-empty marriage. Maybe you've stuffed your life full of other things because of tension at home (your heaven on earth!). I've known many wives who turn to other things—hobbies, classes, church work, volunteer work, running around with girlfriends—to avoid being at home with their husbands. But the truth is that these "other things" are far secondary to the joy and bliss God means for a wife to enjoy with her husband. Therefore, these "other things" will never fill the place that God designed a happy marriage to be.

So why not drop the meaningless peripherals that comprise all your busy-ness? Then put the same time, effort, and energy into doing what God says to do—help your husband, follow your husband, respect your husband, love your husband. You'll be glad you did when the blessings of your obedience to God's guidelines for marriage begin to roll in.

Whatever you do, don't fail to obey! As God's child, you have every power available to you. You have the power of prayer. You have the power of the Holy Spirit. And you have the power of the grace of God (2 Corinthians 12:9). And every form of help is available to you. You have the help of God's Word. You have the help of prayer. You have the help of older women who will assist you, disciple you, mentor you, pray for you, and counsel you (Titus 2:3-5). You have the help of your wise, godly pastor. All of these resources are available to you as you obey God in your roles as a wife. This army of "personal assistants" will help you fine-tune

God's principles to your situation and apply them to your husband.

And whatever you do, don't allow the world to cloud God's view of the importance of your marriage. Don't let anyone sell you on the idea that *anything* (apart from the Lord Himself) is more important than actively nurturing your marriage. God means for our life and our marriages to be filled with passion and purpose. And they can be...if we carefully tend them.

Chapter 8

Managing Your Children

*Behold, children are a heritage from the LORD,
the fruit of the womb is His reward.*
—PSALM 127:3

Children. To me the very word sparkles with life and laughter! From babies to teenagers, children teem with energy. And each one of them represents a life of potential—for our Lord and for mankind. *Nothing* demands that we lean on the Lord more than parenting!

For Jim and me, *having* children did not come easily. And then, when God did grant us the desire of our heart, *raising* children was even more difficult! As I already shared, neither God nor His Word had any place in our lives. So the results were predictable—our home life was chaos! With no "instruction book" and no one to help us, Jim and I stumbled and bumbled our way through not only our marriage, but also our childraising. We were the kind of family you would look at, shake your head, and then point to and say to another couple, "Whatever you do, don't do it like this poor family is doing it!"

But I can never cease to praise and thank God for His work in our lives! When we did become a Christian family, Jim and I had been married eight years and our little girls were almost two and three years old. (That means that for eight years we had been doing our marriage all *wrong,* and for almost three years doing our childraising all *wrong!* That's scary!)

And once again, God…and His wonderful Word…came to our aid. Behold, there were guidelines in the Bible, real principles and do's and don'ts for me to follow as a mother! Little or nothing was left for guesswork.

God's Guidelines for Mothering

Let me share some of the guidelines I found in my annual treks through the Bible. And I want to tell you that I *looked* for them! I looked—eagerly and earnestly…and desperately—for help! I read my Bible each day with a pen in hand. And whenever I found a verse or a passage about mothering or about the mothers of the Bible, I marked it— *boldly!*—in my Bible. And I recorded it. I began to build a set of notes I called "God's Guidelines for Mothering." Here are four of these guidelines.

Teach your children—I know many moms who homeschool their children. But whether you homeschool or not, you are to teach your children. God makes this crystal clear in Deuteronomy 6:6-7:

> And these words which I command you today shall be in your heart. You shall teach them diligently to your children, and shall talk of them when you sit in your house,

when you walk by the way, when you lie
down, and when you rise up.

Who is to teach? Every believing parent! *Who* are you to
teach? Your children! *What* are you to teach? God's Word!
How are you to teach? Diligently! *When* are you to teach? All
day long, every day! *Where* are you to teach? At home and
everywhere!

If you are a mother, teaching your beloved children about
God and His ways is not optional. In Deuteronomy 6 God
is *commanding* you to teach His *commands*…to your children…diligently…all day long, everyday…at home and
everywhere else! Other scriptures also point the teaching
finger directly at us moms (Proverbs 1:8; 6:20; 31:1), but I
think we get the message! We are to teach our children.

Train your children—One verse I wrote down in my
growing list of "guidelines" was Proverbs 22:6. It is a principle that instructs parents to "train up a child in the way he
should go, and when he is old he will not depart from it."
That's the scripture. Therefore, if you have children, you
must train them. As a parent, you are to do the training—
you are to consistently teach God's Word and enforce it with
loving discipline throughout your child's upbringing. Sure,
others may help along the way (godly teachers, mentors,
pastors), but the responsibility is yours.

Your children desperately need your diligent teaching *and*
your faithful training. All children are born sinners, and if
they are allowed to follow their own desires, they will naturally develop sinful habits and practices. And once sinful
habit patterns become deep-seated and ingrained in a child,
they are harder to correct. As clergyman and reformer Henry
Ward Beecher observed, "It is not hard to make a child or a

tree grow right if you train them when they're young, but to make them straighten out after you've allowed things to go wrong is not an easy matter."[1] Therefore, we must "bring them up in the training and admonition of the Lord" (Ephesians 6:4). It's never too early to begin your child's spiritual training. So start now!

Love your children—God's high calling to love your children comes from Titus 2:4. Here the older women in the church are instructed to teach the younger women "to love their children." As with your husband, "Love is the highest blessing in an earthly home, and of this the wife [and mother]…is the natural center."[2] So roll up your mothering sleeves and get to work loving your children. Nurture your love for them. Show them your love. Lavish them with your love! Your loyal love will work wonders in your children's hearts and lives.

Prize your children—Children are a blessing from God! "Behold, children are a heritage from the LORD," and "the fruit of the womb is His reward" (Psalm 127:3). Therefore they are to be prized.

Many women of the Bible "got it" when it came to this guideline of prizing both our children and motherhood.

- *Sarah* wanted and waited for a child for a quarter-century. When her Isaac was finally born, Sarah finally "laughed" with joy (Genesis 21:6).

- *Rebekah* wanted children so badly that her husband Isaac "pleaded with the LORD for his wife, because she was barren" (Genesis 25:21).

- *Rachel* wanted children so badly that she told her husband Jacob, "Give me children, or else I die!" (Genesis 30:1).

- *Hannah* wanted children so badly that she vowed to God that if He would give her a male child, she would "give him to the LORD all the days of his life" (1 Samuel 1:11).

- *Elizabeth* wanted children so badly that she marveled and thanked God when she conceived, saying "He [has] looked on me, to take away my reproach among men" (Luke 1:25).

I'm sure you've heard women talk on and on, complaining from one breath to the next, about the woes of raising children, referring to their little blessings from God as a brat-pack and rug-rats. You see, we've got it all wrong! Children are a blessing. They are an honor bestowed upon us from God. Motherhood is a privilege, and our children are our crowning glory (1 Timothy 2:15).

When I teach women on this vital area of life management—on raising children—I share two illustrations for their shock value. (Well, they shocked me!) The first is about a snail. *The Honolulu Advertiser*[3] reported that a small, brownish, quarter-inch snail on the island of Kauai had been listed as threatened under the Endangered Species Act. In fact, an elaborate recovery plan is being developed by a team of biologists. A snail...a little larger than the head of a nail!

The second story is about an elephant. One morning while Jim and I were sitting on an airplane waiting for takeoff, the television show was reporting on, of all things, elephants. The narrator said that because a female elephant can have a baby only once every four years, each offspring is considered to be priceless.

Now I ask you, how do you feel about *your children*? Each one of them? Do you prize them, protect them, cherish them? Do you consider each of them to be priceless? Animals might be special, but because your children are created in God's image, it's *they* who are truly priceless.

There we have it—the beginning basics for us as mothers: We are to teach our children, to train them, to love them, and to prize them. Now let's look to a new set of disciplines to help us manage as mothers.

Ten Disciplines for Mothering

1.   You shall center your life on the Lord.

Dear mother, *you* are to love the Lord and His Word. *You* are to be a *godly* mother. The verses from Deuteronomy 6 begin, "these words which I command you today shall be in *your* heart" (verse 6). *Then*...you can successfully teach them to your children! You see, consecration must be in the heart—*your* heart—first.

2.   You shall model true godly character.

Mothers can teach and preach their heads off to their children, but if words aren't backed up by godly example, they are simply "sounding brass or a clanging cymbal" (1 Corinthians 13:1). Let's not be the kind of mom whose child one day says, "What you are speaks so loudly I can't hear what you're saying!"

What we are to seek is a life of passion and purpose that is passed on to our children. Hannah (in only a few short years) successfully transmitted—by model and by mouth—

to her little Samuel the foundational truths about God. The same is true of Moses' mother and Timothy's mother (and grandmother!). These godly mothers taught by mouth...but they also modeled by their lives what their children should be before God and man.

Dear reading mom, as Deuteronomy cries out to us, *be* what you are supposed to be so you can *teach* what you are supposed to teach!

3.   You shall pray for your children.

Pray for them generally and individually, one by one, by name and by need. In my first prayer notebook, I had three pages for my children—one marked "Children," one marked "Katherine," and one marked "Courtney." On the general page I prayed for the general requests that covered both girls—salvation, baptism, their times at church camp, their youth pastors, for spiritual growth, for future mates. But on the individual pages, I prayed for their individual needs—their jobs, their friends, their boyfriends(!). (You get the picture!)

4.   You shall be there.

By "there" I, of course, mean at home. Remember again Jesus' principle—"Where your treasure is [in this case, the treasure of your time spent at home with your children], there your heart will be also [in this case your heart will be with your children]" (Matthew 6:21). The more you are with your children, the more opportunities you have to influence their lives. The more you understand them. The more you can train them. The more aware you will be of their friends, their interests, their bent, their personality, their dreams. The

Proverbs 31 mother *watched* "over the ways of her household" (Proverbs 31:27)—that's over the place *and* the people!

We haven't brought up the busy-ness factor for a while, but to be there, to be at home, you'll have to give up lesser things to buy back the time—time at home with your children—that will pay the highest dividends you will ever earn in life.

5. You shall take your children to church.

Make sure your children are exposed regularly to the people of God and the teaching of the Word of God at church. (And don't forget—getting to church begins the night before!)

6. You shall choose your children above all other people and pursuits.

Just as with your husband, your children are your highest priority relationships. When God listed the curriculum the older women in the church are to teach the younger women, the first order of business on the list was "to love their husbands," and the second was "to love their children" (Titus 2:4). Friends, sisters, and the girls at the office didn't make God's top-priority list.

7. You shall discipline your children.

The book of Proverbs teaches us this "discipline" (Proverbs 13:24), along with many ways for correcting and training our children. I saved these tips for disciplining children *many* years ago, and their wisdom still stands.

- Don't compare children with children.
- Don't ridicule or make fun of weaknesses.

- Don't use bribes and rewards.
- Don't withdraw affection from children.
- Don't be afraid to say no.
- Do impart the expectancy of obedience.
- Do help your children plan a better course of action.
- Do allow your children to express their viewpoint.
- Do admit your own parental mistakes.
- Do recognize that discipline is a long-range process.[4]

8. You shall be your children's #1 encourager.

Be your children's biggest fan—the one who always cheers them on, who gives "a word in season" when they are down or suffering (Isaiah 50:4), who comes alongside when they need additional support. Make sure that their days are filled with words of praise and encouragement...from *you!*

9. You shall nurture your marriage.

The best gift you can give your children is to love their father. Remember, too, that once your children are raised, you will still (Lord willing) be a wife! Make sure you nurture your marriage each day.

10. You shall make each day fun.

Where does family "fun" come from? Out of the happy heart of the mother. This book is about management and planning. So plan in some fun with and for your children each day.

I hope this overview gives you a little more information about the direction our mothering must take. I know the road can be rough…and long. More than once you'll wonder if you're going to make it, if you'll ever get there! But oh, the blessings we gather along the way—the memories, the photographs, the many moments of tenderness and love, and most of all, the deposit of truth we are privileged by God to make into the hearts of our offspring! No journey could be more of an adventure. And no road could be more honorable. Be sure you enjoy each and every step of the way!

Looking at Life

As I write this chapter that so scantily touches upon the magnitude of this ever-demanding, top-level priority, I've been a mother for 32 years and am now the grandmother of five little tots. It's true that, if you have children, you are a mother forever. For life! Ages and stages change. The "children" multiply as sons- and daughters-in-law are added… and then their children. On and on the ripples of our godly influence stretch, ebbing their way into the days, weeks, months, years, decades, and centuries. As a Christian, your godly life and your godly mothering sends its shimmering wake throughout all eternity. The impact of your mothering is unmeasurable. Raising your children is life's most difficult assignment, but it is also life's most rewarding. So I beseech you, give mothering all of the passion and purpose it deserves and requires to be done well. Then all the days of your life will be days…and decades…of passion and purpose.

Chapter 9

Managing Your Home

She watches over the ways of her household.
—PROVERBS 31:27

I've just come from standing in front of a bookcase in our family room that has two entire three-foot shelves packed with nothing but books on homemaking! Their titles range from *Hints from Heloise* to *Speed Cleaning*, from *I Hate Housework* to *The Happy Home Handbook*. This library on home management represents my desperate search over the years for H-E-L-P! in yet another all-important area that God means for me to manage.

As you can probably gather from the tales already told about my remedial condition in the marriage and family departments, my status as a homemaker was equally deficient. Oh, my poor family! But once again, God came to my (and their) rescue as I read His Word and cataloged His instructions for maintaining a home with passion and purpose.

God's Guidelines for Homemaking

The Bible is filled with information on the home. What I want to share here are the few guidelines that launched the revolution of my heart...and my home.

Build your home—You don't have to be married to have a home. Indeed, wherever you live is your home. And dear one, you are to *build* it.

- "Wisdom has *built* her house, she has hewn out her seven pillars; she has slaughtered her meat, she has mixed her wine, she has also furnished her table" (Proverbs 9:1-2).

  This may not sound very lovely or seem too appealing. But Solomon is painting a word picture of a spacious and solid home where food and drink aplenty have been painstakingly prepared and literally spread out on a set banqueting table. The place *and* the provisions are described for us. All in all, it's a place where plans have been made, care has been taken, effort has been expended, and the end results are attractive and beneficial. It's a home...a home where the surroundings comfort the soul and the food sustains, nourishes, and energizes the body.

- "Every wise woman *builds* her house, but the foolish pulls it down with her hands" (Proverbs 14:1).

  Rather than using her energy to *tear down* her home, every wise woman devotes herself to building (literally, to *building up*) her home. How do you spend your energy? If you are wise, you'll spend it building and bettering your house. Time is never

110

wasted when you and I use it to create an enhanced environment for our families and for others. Here's a situation where busy-ness is proper, called for, and desperately needed! Don't be guilty of neglecting to busy yourself with your homemaking.

- "Through wisdom a house is *built*, and by understanding it is established; by knowledge the rooms are filled with all precious and pleasant riches" (Proverbs 24:3-4).

  Here's another Solomonic picture—this one focusing on the benefits of building with wisdom, discernment, skill, knowledge, and intelligence. When these qualities are pooled and employed to build a home, the results are predictably pleasant.

What does the word *build* bring to mind? To me it conjures up images of effort, energy, and sweat. It connotes faithfulness (showing up on the job every day). It implies dreaming, then thinking, planning, and organizing so that the dreams become reality. And don't forget attitude! There's a roll-up-your-sleeves mentality that must go with home-building. The tasks must be owned and tackled—and with gusto! The labor must be welcomed—not neglected or despised. Yes, the wise woman (surely you and I!) builds her house. It's her assignment…and she willingly takes on the challenge…with passion and purpose.

Watch over your home—The Proverbs 31 homemaker gives us another guideline—"she *watches over* the ways of her household, and does not eat the bread of idleness" (Proverbs 31:27). She carefully watches over all that goes on in her home. She keeps an eye on everything to do with her house and household. You see, there's a good sense of pride here. It's *her* house, and it's *her* responsibility. So she puts forth much effort and *excels* at her homemaking (verse 29).

Manage your home—In the New Testament Paul wrote that he desired "that the younger widows marry, bear children, *manage* the house" (1 Timothy 5:14). Paul wrote that it was good for these women to have a home to manage, to administrate, to guide, and to preside over. It seems they were idle and lazy...which led to gadding about and excessive visiting...which led to being gossips and busybodies...which led to talking about things which were better left unspoken (verse 13)!

Now, here's a strong, positive case for busy-ness. In this instance, busy-ness is God's cure. Busy-ness is a good thing. It is better to be busy at home than to be a busybody!

Love your home—The King James Version of the Bible says in Titus 2:5 that we women are to be "keepers at home." Other versions of the Bible translate these words as workers at home, homekeepers, good housekeepers, good managers of the household, and home lovers.[1]

I like "home lovers" because I believe that if you love your home, you'll do all the rest. You'll work at building your home and your homemaking. You'll work at keeping your home. You'll work at being a good housekeeper. You'll work at being a good manager of your household.

Both you and I know that love is the world's most powerful motivator. So if we love our home, love being there and love managing it, building it, watching over it, and keeping it, then love will conquer all. No task will be too difficult and no job will be too menial (or meaningless!) but love will enable us and empower us to tackle it, master it, and excel at it (Proverbs 31:29)!

These guidelines from God's Word should turn up the heat of your heart...and your passion...when it comes to God's purpose for you as a woman to manage your home. And now I pray that the following ten disciplines will help to speed you on your way to better home management.

Ten Disciplines for Home Management

As we make our way through these disciplines, remember this: It's not the kind of place or the size of the place you call home, but the tone and the atmosphere of that place that we are seeking to create.

1. You shall be dedicated to managing your home.

I don't just mean committed to the smooth running of your home. No, I mean dedicated! Devoted! Passionate! Managing your home is a spiritual issue. Why? First of all, because the many guidelines we've just read come to us right out of the Bible. These good-housekeeping assignments are shot right from God's heart...to yours.

Plus, how we manage our home is an indicator of our Christian faith. As writer and speaker Elisabeth Elliot observes, "a sloppy life speaks of a sloppy faith." Surely then, a sloppy place or home speaks of a sloppy faith. We are careful in our faith—careful to tend to our spiritual growth, careful to obey God's Word, careful to maintain the spiritual disciplines of prayer, worship, giving, etc. So why shouldn't we be careful about how we manage our home? After all, our

management is a reflection of our relationship with God…
either for good or bad (Titus 2:5).

2. You shall be a woman of prayer.

We already know prayer changes *things*. And dear reader,
prayer changes our housework! How? Because it changes
the heart of the homemaker. As you and I are faithful to pray
about this realm of our work, the principle of Matthew 6:21
again goes into effect—"Where your treasure is [in this case,
the treasure of your time and spiritual effort spent praying
for your home and homemaking], there your heart will be
also." As I so often say, prayer transports your homemaking
out of the physical realm and into the spiritual realm.

3. You shall be aware of the basics.

The basics of food, clothing, cleanliness, and safety are
parts of your responsibility to your family. Just skim through
Proverbs 31:10-31 and count the ways this master manager
ministered to her family by providing for their basic needs.

4. You shall follow a schedule.

I mentioned my many books on homemaking, but I also
have several shelves of books on time management. Almost
every one of these books—on both topics—lists a schedule
as a powerful tool for making progress, for achieving goals,
and for managing your household and your time. When
your days, weeks, months, and years run on a rhythm, your
work at home gets done. And a schedule makes it happen.
Consider again God's Proverbs 31 homemaker. Her day and
her schedule began early, even before her family got up

(verse 15). Then her chores are enumerated as her day progresses.

What I do each evening is make my to-do lists for the next day. I do this as I review my lists for the current day, noting what items were accomplished and which ones were begun. If follow-up is necessary, I place them on my list for the next day with my new items. Then each item gets scheduled into a specific time slot or into three general perimeters—morning, afternoon, or evening. I also keep my eye on a master plan and schedule for the week, the month, and the season. When I'm finished, I have my lists made and each item is scheduled.

Careful scheduling takes care of housework, correspondence, bill-paying, errand-running, meal-planning and preparation, family activities, gardening...the list goes on. I work all day long off of my schedule. I carry it with me everywhere. It never leaves my side. And no, not everything gets done, but more gets done than if I didn't have a schedule!

5.   You shall be organized.

Organization captures the meaning of the age-old principle of a place for everything and everything in its place. (And in advanced organization, that place is the place where you need each item to be.) Whatever the method of organization, and there are many, it always aids the smooth running of a household. Right now my daughter Courtney is working her way through her house using author Emilie Barnes's method of "working like mad" and "cleaning like mad" for 15 minutes a day in one room until it's done, then moving to the next room. I'm working my way through my house by my own method. I call it the "one foot" method. I clean out at least one drawer, one shelf, or one foot of space every day. And it's usually done during transitional time, while I'm doing something else, like warming something in the microwave, waiting for the coffee to brew, heating food on the stove, talking on the phone, etc. There are few feelings that are better than being organized. Whatever the method, have one and be organized.

6. You shall be there.

Exactly how do our good housekeeping chores get done? They get done when we, the homemaker and housekeeper, are there—when we are at home! So look at your calendar for this week. Pinpoint and count exactly how many hours you are scheduled out of the house. Then reduce them drastically so that you can "be there." (Then put your to-do lists into action!)

7. You shall be the best.

I've adopted the Proverbs 31 homemaker as my model for home management. She *excelled* at her role of home-manager (verse 29). My thinking goes something like this—"Okay, I have to keep the house clean. I need to create order. I've got to see to three meals a day. So why not be the best? Why not excel? Why not exceedingly bless my family and others?"

8. You shall be reading.

There's no reason you can't learn about the skills, methods, and tools that make for better homemaking (like reading the Emilie Barnes book I mentioned). Even if you learned nothing about homemaking when you were growing up, all you have to do is read and learn now. Material is everywhere on this subject. At checkout counters. In magazines. Books. Newspapers. Online. Collect it, read it, save it, and do it. If your heart is willing, you can improve by reading.

9.   You shall be frugal.

We have an entire section on finances coming up. But a major gift you give to your homemaking is the frugal management of your household budget. Every penny saved is a penny you can put to use serving your family and others who need your assistance. Thrift and the wise management of money are biblical virtues that bless our family.

10.   You shall be creative.

I love being a homemaker because it gives me many opportunities to learn and master new skills, to excel in the sphere God has set aside for me to manage, and to express my creativity in countless ways. Just think, you and I can be as creative as we like as we paint, sew, cook, garden, decorate, organize, and make crafts. And every one of these ways blesses us, our family, and others. Even if you have a job outside the home, you get to come home to your home-sweet-home and make it even sweeter!

Are you feeling overwhelmed? Please don't! The good news is that creating a heaven on earth inside the door of your home is done one step at a time, one task at a time, one day at a time...beginning with today.

Looking at Life

Think again about the place where you live, the place you call home. You and I have little control over most of the events of our lives. But we do have a measure of control over the atmosphere and the order and the smooth running of our home. You see, what's inside our doors and under our roof is *our* sphere. It's *our* place. By and large, it's a sphere and a place we build, watch over, manage, and love. So why shouldn't we dive in and do it with great passion and purpose?

I know women who have trouble getting excited about taking care of their homes. And I know women who have written off homemaking as a worthless occupation. Does either category fit you, my dear friend? Then please, spend time in prayer. Turn your home...and your heart...over to your all-wise and loving heavenly Father. Ask Him for help. Ask Him for a "make-over"! Look up the scriptures shared in this chapter. Talk to other women who do love taking care of their homes. Ask your husband to encourage you and pray for you. Make your schedule for a week and give a copy of it to someone who will pray for you and hold you accountable for these godly desires of your heart. Whatever it takes, set about to create a heaven on earth where you live.

Part IV

Taking Care of Business

Managing Your
Financial Life

Chapter 10

God's Guidelines
for Your Money

*Seek first the kingdom of God and His righteousness,
and all these things shall be added to you.*
—MATTHEW 6:33

I remember well one day when my husband came home from The Master's Seminary where he served as Dean of Admissions for so many years. On that particular day a young man—a college student—had come by Jim's office to talk about enrolling as a student in the seminary. Well, there was no problem with the man. What a gem! He was a student body officer at a Christian college, a fine scholar, and well thought of by others.

No, this potential pastor had another problem that he wanted to discuss with Jim. A *girl* problem, to be more specific. (Nothing new for Jim!) This man was spending some get-acquainted time with a fellow female student and admitted to being attracted to her. But here was the problem—the young man wanted to know if he should continue to date her...just in case he fell in love with her and might want to marry her. He wanted to know now, because

121

when she graduated from college she would be personally in debt for $22,000 for her education. His eyes were wide open to the fact that if things progressed, he, a minister-to-be, might find himself married to a woman with a large debt. He knew such a liability would be a heavy burden to carry and a blight on his credit report. But he had an even greater concern—what church or mission organization would call a man who was deeply in debt to lead its congregation?

My dear reading sister, do you ever wonder how in the world financial matters could matter in your life? Or how *your* financial matters could matter in the lives of others? Well, this is a real-life scenario. You see, no matter how young (the girl in question was not even 21) or how old we are, God has given us yet another area of life to manage for Him, for His glory, and according to His principles. And that area is our finances. Our money. Money may not sound like a spiritual responsibility, but it is. In fact, it was Jesus who taught us in one of His parables, "He who is faithful in what is least is faithful also in much; and he who is unjust in what is least is unjust also in much" (Luke 16:10).

Following God's guidelines for finance will definitely help us to not only faithfully manage our money, but also live each day with passion and purpose. Let's look at just a few of those guidelines now.

You Are a Steward

As with all areas of our lives, we are to be faithful stewards with our finances. Any money that we have is not ours (contrary to popular belief!). It is God's (Job 1:21). And we are to manage it *for* Him. Furthermore, *how* we manage it is of great interest to Him. In yet another of Jesus' parables, the owner of an estate, before going on a trip, gave three of his servants differing amounts of money. When the master returned he wanted to know *exactly* what each servant had done with *his* money (Matthew 25:14-30), and he rewarded—or chastised—them accordingly. The two who were "faithful" with a few things were given the stewardship of many more things. However, the one who was unfaithful (Jesus described him as wicked and lazy) was rebuked and stripped of what he did have.

Assessing your stewardship—Now, dear one, what do *you* have that God has entrusted to you? What do *you* have that God expects you to manage for Him? For instance...

Are you married? Has God given you a man to take care of for Him? Has He given you a marriage to nurture?

And do you have children? How many? Do you see each and every one of those precious children as a gift God has given you to take care of for Him? To raise in the nurture and admonition of the Lord? To teach His Word to?

And where do you live? In a home? In an apartment? In a trailer? In a hut on the mission field? Well, my friend, wherever it is, once again, it's yours to manage and take care of for the Lord. Married or single, we live *some*where. And that somewhere has been entrusted to us from the mind and hand of God.

We could go on and on with the many elements of life that you (and I) must manage for God—our ministry, our spiritual giftedness, our education, our credentials. But the focus of this chapter is on our finances. And always, when it comes to our finances, the issue is not how much we have, but how faithful we are as stewards of what we do have. We'll look at some practicalities of money management later, but for now, just allow the concept of stewardship to sink into your understanding of every area of your life.

Meet someone who managed her money well—God's Proverbs 31 woman teaches us many a lesson on management, and we'll visit her often. In fact, be sure to read her remarkable story of diligence in Proverbs 31:10-31. But for now, take away a life-lesson from her life of passion and purpose: She was a wise money manager. From her life we learn about the value of a working knowledge of personal finances. And today, too, we need to know how to pay bills, manage a checkbook, reconcile a bank statement, nurture savings and investments, and hold the reins in on those credit cards.

When I first encountered the Proverbs 31 woman (about 30 years ago), her life- and money-management skills motivated me to ask Jim to teach me the ins and outs of our family finances. Under Jim's tutelage I learned the basics of personal finance. I learned to be a steward. As a result, I've given Jim back hours of time every week for these many years—hours he can spend on other responsibilities at work, at the church, and at home. (Plus I like to think that I've even saved us a little money by assuming some of the watch-care and stewardship in this area of our life.)

Your God Will Provide for All Your Needs

I know that *you* know that *God* takes care of all our needs. (And please note—that's all our *needs*, not all our *wants!*) As the Bible explains, we should be content if we have these two basics—food and clothing (1 Timothy 6:8). In fact, the Bible is full of promises concerning life's needs and God's provision. For instance,

- Jesus preached that we are not to worry about food, clothing, or length of life. Instead, we are to "seek first the kingdom of God and His righteousness, and *all* these things [including the food and clothing!] shall be added to you" (Matthew 6:33).

- The apostle Paul wrote these words to teach and to comfort the Philippians—"My God shall supply *all* your need according to His riches in glory by Christ Jesus" (Philippians 4:19).

- David declared, "I have not seen the righteous forsaken, nor his descendants begging bread" (Psalm 37:25). God put it this way: Whatever the need, "Call upon Me in the day of trouble; I will deliver you" (Psalm 50:15).

- And my favorite is, again from Paul—"God is able to make *all* grace abound toward you, that you, *always* having *all* sufficiency in *all* things, have an abundance for *every* good work" (2 Corinthians 9:8).

Assessing your trust in the Lord—How well do you manage when it comes to the trust department? Do you trust the Lord to take care of your need for food and clothing...or do you live in fear that perhaps He won't? Do you trust God to supply leadership, instruction, encouragement, protection, strength, love, safety, and friendship along life's way...or do you fret about some perceived failure on God's part to truly provide for you? Always remember that God is your Good Shepherd, who promises that you shall not ever want...for anything (Psalm 23:1).

Dear sister-in-Christ, if you are single, God will provide. If you are married, God will provide. If you are childless, God will provide. If you are the mother of 11 (like a woman I recently met in New York), God will provide. If you are in poor health, God will provide. If you are a widow, God will provide. And when you are on your deathbed, God will provide. You can trust in Him, relax in Him, and enjoy the rest that faith provides.

Meet someone who failed to trust in God's provision—The Proverbs 31 woman feared and revered the Lord and trusted in Him (Proverbs 31:30). However, Eve sadly provides us with an example of a woman who failed to trust God for His provision (Genesis 3:1-6). Imagine…living in the Garden of Eden! Imagine…everything you would ever need being right at your fingertips! That's where—and how—Eve lived her daily life. If you're like me, you're probably thinking, "Wow! I could certainly live each day with passion and purpose in surroundings like that. No problem!"

But for Eve, God's above-and-beyond provision wasn't enough. The serpent slithered into her paradise one day and planted a new kind of seed in the Garden—a seed of doubt. He queried Eve with questions like this one—"Has God indeed said, 'You shall not eat of every tree of the garden'?" (Genesis 3:1). Doubt sank its roots even deeper as the serpent, pointing to the one tree God had instructed Eve not to eat from, hissed, "God knows that in the day you eat of it your eyes will be opened, and you will be like God" (verse 5).

Well, that did it! Doubt blossomed into an ugly flower. And Eve decided that God was not "meeting all her needs." So Eve, the mother of us all, broke the one restriction God had placed on her eating habits—she ate from the one and only forbidden tree in the entire Garden of Eden.

Beloved, are you one who knows the promises of God… and believes them? The next time you are tempted to think that God is not "meeting all your needs," remember this— He *is*, whether it looks like it or not. Put your faith to work!

Faith is defined as "the substance of things hoped for, the evidence of things not seen" (Hebrews 11:1). Faith is lived out in a confident assurance of the things hoped for and a certainty of the things we do not see.

So the question is, dear heart, "Do you believe God will provide for all your needs?"

And faith looks up and exclaims, "Of course!"

You Are Called to Contentment

I am blessed to know a beautiful-inside-and-out woman whose number-one message to women is simply, "How to Be Content." I wish you could hear her speak on this subject. And more than that, I wish you could meet her. She's single. She's been involved in full-time ministry for the 30 years I've known her. And she's completely content and totally fulfilled. Her face truly shines with her complete, all-sufficient joy—and contentment—in the Lord.

There's no doubt that contentment is a real tough issue for women. But the Word of God calls us as women who desire to live each and every day with passion and purpose to be content. Paul, the man of God who tells us that "godliness with contentment is great gain" and that food and clothing are all we need to be content (1 Timothy 6:6,8), also gives us these instructions on contentment from his own life:

> I have *learned* in whatever state I am, to be content: I know how to be abased, and I know how to abound. Everywhere and in all things I have *learned* both to be full and to be hungry, both to abound and to suffer need (Philippians 4:11-12).

Contentment is a pearl of great price…and an all-but-extinct virtue. Contentment is also the greatest blessing you and I can enjoy in this world. But, as one playwright comments, "God hath made none contented."[1] This means, dear one, that we've got to do as the apostle Paul encourages us— we've got to *learn* to be content. And Paul tells us how:

- *Contentment is learned*—Twice the great and mighty Paul says he *learned* to be content! This gives us hope and encouragement. Contentment is not something that comes automatically with salvation. And contentment is not a fruit of the Spirit which we enjoy when we are walking in the Spirit. No, contentment is *learned!*

- *Contentment is required when you have much*—Does this sound strange? I mean, wouldn't you think that having much would cause you to be content? Well, the answer is no. In fact, having much can breed a strong desire and lust to have even more. I personally like the advice of John Wesley—"When I have any money I get rid of it as quickly as possible, lest it find a way into my heart."[2]

- *Contentment is required when you have little*—Do you ever erroneously think, "If I just had a little more, I'd be content"? As I said, this is erroneous. It just isn't true! One secret to contentment is what I call the "Just-Enough Prayer" from Proverbs 30:7-9:

  Two things I request of You (deprive me not before I die): …Give me neither poverty nor riches—Feed me with the food You prescribe

for me; lest I be full and deny You, and say,
"Who is the LORD?" Or lest I be poor and
steal, and profane the name of my God.

Whenever I speak to women on contentment, I try to
allow time for this "Just-Enough Prayer." Note that the
ingredients in this recipe call for just "enough."

A Recipe for Contentment

Health enough to make work a pleasure;
Wealth enough to support your needs;
Strength enough to battle with difficulties
  and forsake them;
Grace enough to confess your sins and
  overcome them;
Patience enough to toil until some good is
  accomplished;
Charity enough to see some good in your
  neighbor;
Love enough to move you to be useful and
  helpful to others;
Faith enough to make real the things of
  God;
Hope enough to remove all anxious fears
  concerning the future.[3]

- *Contentment is not based on your present circumstances*—You and I possess all the true riches of heaven—both here on earth and held in trust for us in heaven to come. We have the hope of eternal life... no matter what is currently going on in our life. Life *is* tribulation (John 16:33)! But we can have peace of

129

mind and contentment of soul *in the midst of* our present circumstances. Why? Because…

- *Contentment is based on the person of God* (Philippians 4:13,19)—As a popular song title reminds us about God, "All That I Need Is All That You Are." In God, precious one, you and I have all that we need—both now and forever!

Assessing your contentment—That's quite a list of truths, isn't it? Would those who know you best think of you as a contented woman? Would they say that your very countenance radiates a spirit that is undisturbed? A spirit that is untroubled by the wants and needs of life? A spirit that is pleased with what it does have as well as what it doesn't have? Or are you one who might be described as having a "murmuring spirit"? A spirit that is rarely satisfied, rarely at rest, rarely content in the Lord and in His provision? Think about it. And be honest, because your approach to your financial life will be determined by your level of contentment…which is determined by your trust in God. To live each day with passion and purpose, you simply cannot be bothered by the things of this world. There just isn't enough time or energy in a day for you to waste even a second or a thought—let alone your emotions—on even one discontented thought.

Meet someone who was truly content—Are you ready to meet one of my favorite women in the Bible? I wish I could tell you her name, but she is nameless. We know her simply as "the Shunammite woman." She provides us with a wonderful picture of what contentment looks like, forever framed in 2 Kings 4:8-17. The Shunammite woman, a warm, caring, and generous person, was used by God to provide room and board for His prophet Elisha. She was married but had no children.

When Elisha asked this "great" woman (KJV) what he could do for her to repay her many kindnesses to him and his servant, the noble Shunammite woman answered with words to this effect, "Why, nothing! I'm perfectly content. Nothing about my life disturbs me. I live with my own people. What more could I possibly want or need?"

That's it, precious one. She "got it"…and may you and I do the same. May we mirror this dear woman's sweet heart of contentment. And may we seek to spend our days doing as Paul did—*learning* to be content in any and all circumstances. Then, perhaps by God's good grace, we will gain what one Puritan writer called "the rare jewel of Christian contentment."[4] And what an exquisite jewel it is!

Looking at Life

As I'm sitting here at my desk reading over the scriptures I've shared in this chapter and reflecting upon these "rudiments of money management," I'm aware that I've said nothing about actual money management. I've written nothing about ledger sheets, debits, credits, nickels, dimes, and dollars. No. We've been addressing the matter of the *heart*. We've been going over our God-entrusted stewardship of all that we have and all that we are. We've been looking deep into our hearts at how much we do or don't trust God to lovingly provide for us. We've been admiring and desiring that fine jewel of godly contentment.

And why? Why go over these deeper issues? Because the first thing we must manage is our heart. As Christian women, our hearts and our lives (and everything else!)

belong to God. And when our affections are set on God, everything else falls into place…even (and maybe especially) so crass an everyday matter as money.

So, dear heart, as the sacred hymn calls to us, we must *turn* our eyes upon Jesus. *That's* what this chapter's been all about. Because then and only then will "the things of earth will grow strangely dim in the light of His glory and grace."[5] And then and only then will the passion and purpose of our life be *Him*…and nothing but Him. And, oh, what a life *that* will be!

Ten Disciplines
for Managing Your Money

*For where your treasure is,
there your heart will be also.*
—MATTHEW 6:21

Do you remember the young 20-year-old college student with large school loans I told you about at the beginning of our last chapter? Well, now let me introduce you to another woman, a woman who lived her life on the other end of the spectrum in every way. That woman is Jim's mother. Oh, what a saint! Our family (and all who knew her) were blessed by the 76 years of Lois's life.

We were blessed, first of all, by how Lois lived her life. She had two passions (and purposes)—her Lord and her family. She loved God, and she loved her family. She served God, and she served her family. If ever a woman had God at the center of her life, it was Lois! She not only loved God, but also managed her life according to His principles. And that included the financial area of her life. Married to an unbelieving husband, Lois still found ways to give money to her church regularly. Not only that—she gave to missionaries, to the needy, and to her church charities. On and on her giving went.

But our family was also blessed by how Lois died. While the cancer that took her life was cruel and ugly, Lois's death was a lesson in beauty to us. Up to her last conscious minutes, Lois was busy giving her money away. She never had much. In fact, she was pretty much the living definition of a poor widow. In the end, Lois was living in a one-bedroom apartment in a retirement center for senior citizens. She had shopped and found the one that gave her the most, yet cost the least. As we went through her finances later, we noticed that the money she gave every month to her church was more than her monthly rent bill! (Now, there's a principle worth following!)

On and on Lois's life of giving went—to the church, to her favorite ministries (both at home and around the world). Why, she even met with each of our daughters before she died to give them a lump sum amount. They were struggling newlyweds at the time, and she knew exactly how to help them out. And when Lois finally went to be with the Lord, she had given all of her money away.

Plus her possessions were down to a minimum. When we cleaned out Lois's tiny apartment, we all expressed, in one way or another, "This is the way we should all live!" She had already sorted through everything she owned, pared it all down, and dispensed with most of it. And what was left (and that wasn't very much) was filed, organized, packed, and labeled. Even her bank accounts had been closed out and transferred to Jim. There was nothing left undone, there were no matters for us to deal with, there were no unpaid bills or debts, and there were no loose ends. No, Lois had managed every area of her life wisely. She had also lived out what one saint of old desired when he wrote, "I should not like to meet God with a full bank account."

Ten Disciplines for Managing Your Money

As you and I seek to manage the financial element of our life *God's* way and for *God's* purposes (like our dear Lois did), these time-honored truths from His Word are sure guidelines for us.

1. You shall not be in debt.

The Bible is right when it says "the borrower is servant to the lender" (Proverbs 22:7). Yet another scripture tells us we are to "owe no one anything" (Romans 13:8). Being in debt is a form of bondage. It also causes you to live your life under a dark and heavy cloud, stifling your freedom to truly enjoy life and to give to those who need help or who serve God. Here are a few tried-and-true ways to make inroads against any debt you may have incurred.

✓ Go on a "fast." By that I mean cease all unnecessary spending. Determine to go a month without frivolous purchases. That means no eating out. No little doo-dads for the house. As a family we've done this in our household more times that I care to recall. And it's always so refreshing. It's like stopping to take a deep, satisfying breath of fresh air. It clears your vision. It purges your covetous soul. It opens your eyes to the needs of others. It gives you a renewed appreciation of all that God is faithful to bless you with. It gives you a new strength—the strength gained through any discipline—for facing and dealing with every other part of your life. It gives birth to a greater measure of self-control. It brings about sort of a Spartan mentality—an attitude of no nonsense, no frills. It fosters a bare-bones, clear-headed, frugal approach to life. It breeds a mean-and-lean outlook on life.

✓ Pray instead of spending. Start a prayer list concerning the items you think you need. Perhaps put each need on a 3" x 5" card. Then look at the cards often. Pray over them daily (...more often, if necessary). Carry them with you in case you need to add more items. Pray for the patience to wait for God to meet your real needs. Then three blessings are accomplished. First, you enjoy a spiritual victory over temptation. Second, you not only didn't *add* to your indebtedness, but actually made advancements toward *subtracting* from your debt (that is, *if* you apply the money not spent toward present debt!). And third, God is glorified when *He* provides for you instead of you rushing to provide for yourself by going into debt.

✓ Maximize short-term strategies. If you need some quick money, then rather than buy new food, use up what's in the pantry and cupboards. (Our family did this—often!) Gather together unneeded possessions in your home and have a garage or yard sale. And here's another short-term strategy—just say no. Every *no* to purchasing anything is quick money. Why? Because money not spent is money you still have! Also, give up expensive habits like your daily latte or eating out. (Again, every no to a habit is quick money.)

2. You shall not spend more than you make.

In my research for this chapter I uncovered these danger signals that usually indicate financial problems. You and your family are in danger when you...

- Use a substantial amount (20 percent or more) of take-home pay to pay off credit card debts.
- Add new debts before paying off old ones.
- Have consistent outstanding debts with banks or lending companies.
- Are frequently late on payments.
- Are continuing to stretch out your debts for longer periods of time.[1]

The problem is obvious, isn't it? If you are in this kind of situation, you are spending more money than you and/or your husband make.

3. You shall not buy on credit.

The two general guidelines Jim and I follow for buying on credit are these: First, having a mortgage is okay when purchasing a home, since a home is considered an investment and an asset. And second, using a credit card is okay only if we pay off our credit card purchases in full each month. Otherwise buying on credit is pretty much out.

An image from Scripture that helps Jim and me hold the line when it comes to buying on credit is forever burned in our minds. From Proverbs 22:27, it warns, "If you have nothing with which to pay, why should [your creditor] take away your bed from under you?" In other words, if you can't afford to pay in full for something, why take the risk of having your very furniture taken out from under you and removed from your house? Why risk suffering the discomfort...and shame...of being unable to pay for items you can't afford?

4.   You shall not covet what others have.

"Keeping up with the Joneses" has long been the American way of life. But our goal in life as Christian women who long to live our lives unto the Lord should be far different. Our goal should be to follow God's disciplines, not to love *the world* and the *things* of this world (1 John 2:15)—and that includes the things of the Joneses!)—but to instead seek first and foremost *the kingdom of God* and His righteousness (Matthew 6:33). Beloved, you and I don't have to keep up with anyone! We have only to live for the Lord, to live for His purposes, and to live according to His principles.

5.   You shall not love money.

Contrary to Mark Twain's quip "The lack of money is the root of all evil," the Bible says "the *love* of money is a root of all kinds of evil" (1 Timothy 6:10). Loving money can lead to all kinds of evils and vices. (Maybe that's why one version of the Bible calls money "filthy lucre"—1 Timothy 3:3 [KJV].) Perhaps the worst evil the love of money can lead to is a waning affection for the Lord and the things of the Lord.

Again, "where your treasure is, there your heart will be also" (Matthew 6:21). This fact of life, as we've noted, was spoken by Jesus, who then went on to give us yet another fact of life—"No one can serve two masters; for either he will hate the one and love the other, or else he will be loyal to the one and despise the other. You cannot serve God and mammon" (verse 24).

Beloved, these are strong words, but true. We either love money and hate our Master…or we hate money and love our Master. We simply cannot love money *and* love the Master! It will always be one or the other. Perhaps that's why John Chrysostom, one of the early fathers of the church, wrote in around A.D. 400, "Let us despise money."

6.   You shall give regularly to your church.

The Bible is very clear on this "discipline." Paul wrote quite specifically to those in the church at Corinth about the regularity of giving—"on the first day of the week" (that's Sunday) everyone was to set aside some amount of money to give to the Lord (1 Corinthians 16:2).

And our giving is to be purposeful—"Let each one give as he purposes in his heart" (2 Corinthians 9:7). I like the translation of this verse that reads, "Let everyone give as his heart tells him."[2] You see, God weighs the *heart*, not the offering. God is more concerned about the giver than about the gift. We shouldn't just drop some money into the offering plate. We are instructed to *think* about our giving, to *pray* about an amount, to search our *heart* about our motives (the heart is deceitful and desperately wicked, you know!—Jeremiah 17:9), to make a *decision*, and then to give it…regularly, prayerfully, and purposefully.

7.   You shall give generously.

We are also to give generously, to "abound" in the grace of giving (2 Corinthians 8:7). And along with this abounding generosity and grace of giving should come an element of cheerfulness. Again, Paul writes to let us know that we are not to give "grudgingly or of necessity; for God loves a cheerful giver" (2 Corinthians 9:7). Here's a "cheerful" picture of giving—imagine yourself, when you give your offering or your contribution, exuberantly flinging it into the sky. Imagine yelling out as you fling it heavenward, "Here it is, Lord! Thank You, Lord! I love You, Lord! Next week I hope there's even more to give to You!"

Obviously there are many *ways* (right and wrong) to give—cheerfully, gladly, grudgingly, reluctantly, or with pain or constraint. And there are many *places* to give. But there's no doubt that giving to your church is vitally important to God—so important that He included detailed instructions for us in the Bible about it. So this discipline of giving to the church should be the first we tend to.

But beyond giving to our church, I also work hard on nurturing a generous spirit, what the Bible calls "a liberal soul" (Proverbs 11:25 KJV). Again, the Proverbs 31 woman shows me a model. She, like our Lord, went about doing good (Acts 10:38). Her generous heart is described in this way—"She extends her hand to the poor, yes, she reaches out her hands to the needy" (Proverbs 31:20). Her eyes... and her heart...and her hands...were open, and whatever the need, she rushed to give.

I can still vividly remember the day I began praying every morning on my daily walk to be more generous. You see, I had assessed my spiritual life and the seven areas of life management we are covering in this book. And I had found myself seriously lacking in this area of generosity. So I decided to begin praying about it every day. I now ask God daily to help me listen for opportunities to give, to open my eyes and my heart, and to bring to my knowledge the needs of others. So I "purposed" (as Paul suggested) to make this grace a regular part of my daily life. I don't consider this "works." I consider this fine-tuning my heart to God's Word, God's ways, God's grace, and to the needs of others.

I wish I could tell you of the many spiritual blessings my husband and I have received since I (Jim has never had a problem with stinginess! His "problem" has always been one of being overly generous, if there is such a problem!) set about to remedy a failure in this grace of giving. These blessings will ever remain secret, but oh, I know what they are... and my Lord knows...as do some who have been helped along the way.

8.   You shall know your financial condition at all times.

When it comes to your finances, believe me, ignorance is *not* bliss! How in the world can we manage our finances as stewards for the Lord if we don't even know where we stand or what we've got—or not got? I've met mothers of newborns who carefully record in a notebook the exact time their infant eats and how much and for how long. I've also met women who are on a serious weight reduction plan who strictly and unwaveringly follow the instructions from their "coach" to write down the time they eat and the amount of every morsel that goes into their mouth, along with mathematical calculations of the number of calories consumed.

Dear sister, this kind of careful attention is called for with any discipline. Managing our money, like all other disciplines, starts with a daily working knowledge of our financial condition.

Here's how it goes for me. I weigh myself every morning. Then I go a step further—I write down my weight in my daily planner *and* in my personal journal. Then I know how

I'm doing. My weight is either going up, down, or I'm holding the line. And that's either good or bad, depending on my specific goals at the time. But by weighing myself every day I know at the outset of each day whether to watch my eating more carefully or if I'm doing okay. I also know the trend my weight is taking.

Well, I do the same thing with our family finances. I get on-line every morning and check our bank balance. (And if you don't use your computer and the Internet, you can always keep track in your checkbook or dial your bank's toll-free customer banking line, and get a recording of your balances.) Either way, I write our balance down in a small spiral banking notebook with each day's date. It's the same thing as keeping track of my weight—I know how we're doing financially. Our balances are either going up, down, or we're holding the line. And that's either good or bad, depending on our specific goals at the time. But by knowing our financial condition every day, I know at the outset of each day whether to watch our spending more carefully or if we're doing okay. I also know the trend our money management (or lack of!) is taking.

9. You shall have a reserve.

This is a very practical principle for your finances. As John Wesley wrote regarding money, "Make all you can, save all you can, give all you can." That's a good balance. Make all you can—the Bible is clear that we are to work, and to work hard. Save all you can—we live in very uncertain times and some money in reserve for hard times is a principle of wisdom. Oliver Wendell Holmes put it this way—"Put not your trust in money, but put your money in trust."[3] And give all you can—I think we're already on our way here!

10. You shall practice self-control.

Self-control is defined as self-mastery, self-restraint, as holding self in and/or back. Thank God that He has given us the grace-gift of His self-control (Galatians 5:23). It's one of the fruit of the Spirit. When we obey God's command to walk in the Spirit (verse 16) and look to Him for His self-control over our fleshly desires, then He enables us to rein in those desires. Then we can live out *His* plan for our life; we can live our life *His* way, in a way that glorifies Him...because it is *Him* living *His* life through us.

Looking at Life

In case you haven't noticed, I'm coming in the back door to the details and the how-to's of managing this area of your financial life. But there's a reason. You can know all there is to know about bookkeeping, budgeting, record-keeping, reconciling your bank statements, savings accounts, CDs, interest rates, IRAs, pension plans, etc. You can also possess the ability (or grace) to say no, to hold the line on your spending, to live frugally. But if you fail to know the *purpose* for managing your money, then you'll never have a *passion* about it.

And that passion, my dear reading friend and sister-in-Christ, is what we're aiming at in this book. Have you sensed it yet? Have you caught the vision? Is the purpose looming large and clear before your heart and soul? And is the passion beginning to burn brighter and hotter?

We simply can't be lackadaisical about this matter of money. It's not *ours!* It's *God's!* And how we manage it *for* Him is a measure of our spiritual maturity. And it's another discipline that makes us the women we want to be—godly women, women who live for God, women who love Him supremely, women who love Him enough to take care of the business of the resources He so graciously hands us.

I know you're busy. That's why you picked up a book with the title this one bears—*Life Management for Busy Women.* But, my friend, you *cannot* be too busy to neglect an assignment your Lord is giving to you—managing your finances for His glory. Being a woman with no ties to money. Being a woman who has no other gods (especially the god of money) before Him. Being a woman with a healthy take-it-or-leave-it attitude of contentment when it comes to having and/or loving money. Being a woman who can live with it or without it. Being a woman who has a neutral heart in the area of affection for worldly riches.

Let's leave this chapter with this thought for living life: No *person* is really dedicated to God until that person's *money* is dedicated to God.

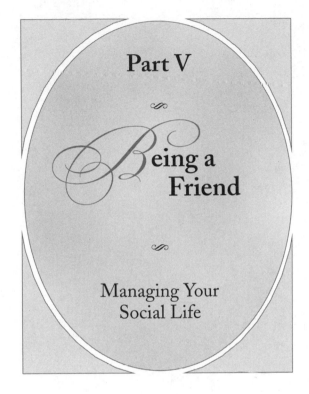

Part V

Being a
Friend

Managing Your
Social Life

Chapter 12

God's Guidelines
for Your Friendships

*A friend loves at all times,
and a brother is born for adversity.*
—PROVERBS 17:17

One day this past week I found myself tilting toward frustration over the slew of interruptions in my day. I definitely wasn't managing well. So I decided to jot down something about each of the intrusions on my personal plan for my precious day to see what might be going on.

Well, my time log was quite revealing. Do you know what the day's number-one hitch was? It was people!

For starters, our phone rings...a lot. And, amazingly, there's always a person on the other end of the line! And on the day I'm detailing for you, our household received a number of incoming phone calls (which means we had a number of people to talk to on the phone). In addition to incoming calls, both Jim and I made several outgoing calls... to more people. There were phone calls to doctors, to friends who are suffering, to family members both near and far, to people in our church and in other churches, to airlines, to department stores, to computer help lines. On and on the list went. (You know the scene.) Plus on this particular day we had neighbors stopping by, friends dropping in, family getting together, and the college women from church who came to the house for a chili supper. And these are only the encounters with people *at* our home!

Then there were the meetings with people *outside* our home—the clerks at the post office, the girls at the beauty shop, the man at the cleaners. Just another typical day, right?

There's no doubt that people make up a substantial part of life and account for much of our busy-ness. Our social encounters on every level are something that we must manage, and hopefully manage God's way!

In this book about busy-ness it's high time we addressed the time we spend with people. You and I are social beings. Our need for companionship and fellowship stems from the creation of man. As early as Genesis 2—the second chapter in the Bible—God said, "It is not good that man should be alone; I will make him a helper comparable to him" (verse 18). Here we have the beginnings of a social unit—a couple. Then God instructed this first couple, Adam and Eve, the first two people on the earth, to multiply and fill the earth...with other social beings—a family.

On the heels of Genesis we read in the book of Exodus—the second book in the Bible—the Ten Commandments God handed down to mankind. Did you know that six of the Ten Commandments listed in Exodus 20 deal with social relationships? And God has not only given us His *commandments* for our friendships and relationships, but He has also given us a few other guidelines. As you look at these guidelines, you'll notice I've broken them down into three categories—friendships with family, friendships within the family of God, and friendships outside the church.

Friendships with Family

The first category of friendships centers on the family, which was instituted in Genesis 2:18. It all began with...

Marriage—If you are married, your marriage partner is to be your first concern. Your husband is to receive your first and largest investment of time and effort when it comes to friendships and managing your social life. We've already discussed God's instructions to us as wives to see that we love our husbands (Titus 2:4). We now know that this is friendship love. We are to love our husbands as our best friends, as cherished brothers, as intimate mates. We listened to what the bride of King Solomon said of her new husband— "This is my beloved, and this is my friend" (Song of Solomon 5:16). Could you sing this same song about your feelings toward your dear husband?

And there are other couples in the Bible who show us the friendship bond that should be found in a marriage. Eve and her Adam stuck together through the good and bad times of sin and life. As the first two people, all they had was each other...and their friendship...to see them through.

Elizabeth and Zacharias were marriage partners who weathered life and its difficulties together. Childless into their senior years together, they never wavered in their devotion to one another and to God. Through the bad and the bitter, they remained "righteous before God, walking in all the commandments and ordinances of the Lord blameless" (Luke 1:6).

Sarah and Abraham probably set the record when it comes to longevity in marriage and the years of life and problems endured together. This godly couple "left and cleft" home, family, and friends to obey God's command to

Abraham to "get out of your country, from your kindred, and from your father's house, to a land that I will show you" (Genesis 12:1). Their obedience led to a lifetime of wandering through foreign lands, not knowing where they were going, of dwelling in tents and encountering dangerous enemies. This couple also had no children…until Sarah was 90 years old and Abraham was a hundred. They give new meaning to the familiar sentiment of "Come grow old with me"!

Dear sister, if you are married, friendship with your husband should be a goal and a priority. Maybe something has happened in your marriage that has distanced the two of you. And now that long-lost friendship seems impossible to revive and looks too difficult or too hopeless to regain. But ask God through prayer to work first in *your* heart. Ask for His forgiveness of any hardness in your heart. And ask Him to help you *want* to be your husband's companion and friend. Then as you work on managing your busy life so your husband's portion of the friendship pie is the largest, ask God to work in your *husband's* heart. After all, weren't you best friends at one time? Why not seek to rekindle that friendship? (And don't forget…where your treasure is, there will your heart also be.)

Children—In a prior chapter we considered God's instruction that we women are to love our husbands *and* love our children (Titus 2:4). We also noted that spending time with girlfriends didn't make the list of things older Christian women are to teach younger women. These other relationships have a place in our lives…but not a prominent place. The choice places are reserved for our husbands and our children. And we are to manage our time and our friendships accordingly.

When you think of the opportunity we have as mothers to impact (by God's grace and with His ever-needed assistance) the world for Jesus Christ by setting our hearts and minds and energies and efforts—and time—to work raising (Lord willing) another generation of Christians, it's staggering! Think for a minute about these godly mothers of the Bible.

Moses' mother gave her time and her soul to her children...and in doing so gave God and the world Moses, Aaron, and Miriam. These three led God's people out of Egypt and through the wilderness to the Promised Land.

Hannah, Samuel's mother, gave her time, her prayers, and her devotion to prepare her little Samuel for a life of service to God (1 Samuel 1-2). He became God's great prophet, priest, leader, and judge.

Solomon was Bathsheba's "beloved." He was "the son of her vows" and the object of her most pious efforts and devotion to God (Proverbs 31:2). Her beloved Solomon became the wisest man who ever lived before Jesus Christ.

John the Baptist's mother was Elizabeth. Her at-long-last son, John, became the forerunner of Jesus, and a passionate preacher who paved the way for Messiah. When he was murdered, Jesus said of him, "there has not risen one greater than John the Baptist" (Matthew 11:11).

Timothy was the product of God's use of a mother-grandmother team, Lois and Eunice. From childhood he was taught the Holy Scriptures (2 Timothy 3:15) and became a "son," a brother, and a teammate to Paul as they ministered together for Christ.

I hope you will write to me if you can think of even one woman in the Bible whose friendship with another woman (outside of kin) is mentioned in the Bible. You see, family was everything. These women's lives centered on building their homes and on building their relationships with the people at home. And their hearts were set on training their children to love, follow, and serve the Lord.

Certainly things have changed! But the priority, the focus, the heartbeat of the days of our lives, must be on our loved ones—our husbands, our children, our grandchildren. Precious mother, when you die what do you want to leave behind? A club membership? A gaggle of girlfriends? A few bridge buddies? Golfing partners? Or...your precious lifeblood, your child who became your friend and a friend of God? What mark do you want to leave on the world? How about the mark of a child who marks the world for Christ? How about another on-fire, passionate heart that burns for Christ and will, in turn, light the torch, God willing, of yet another generation of Christians?

Priceless mom, watch your priceless time! Be sure it's spent in the best place and on the best pursuit—your child's priceless heart. Even if your beloved one has erred and failed to follow Christ, never give up. Never quit. Never fail to nurture your friendship. Give your all, all that it takes and all the time and all the prayer you can utter. Never forget that "love suffers long and is kind; love...bears all things, believes all things, hopes all things, endures all things. Love never fails" (1 Corinthians 13:4,7-8). Who knows what God may do?

Parents and siblings—Another strong link to be forged in the social chain is also made up of family—your parents, in-laws, siblings, and extended family. They, too, are to receive a significant portion of the pie of your time and attention.

First, our parents. The Bible is full of teachings about the respect and honor parents are due because of their position. The teaching that we hear most often comes from Ephesians

6:2-3—"'Honor your father and mother,' which is the first commandment with promise: 'that it may be well with you and you may live long on the earth.'" The internal quote marks point out words that are quoted directly from the Ten Commandments (Exodus 20:12). Obviously God is interested in our relationship with our parents.

I cannot say strongly enough that we as Christian women must nurture our relationship with our parents. And, if we're married, the same attention must be given to our husband's parents. These family connections, ordained by God, are important to Him. Nurturing them is not optional. No, it is commanded. And our spiritual maturity is revealed by whether or not we get along with parents and in-laws. God has given us all the grace (2 Corinthians 12:9) and all the love (Galatians 5:22) and all the resources (2 Peter 1:3) we need to get along with anyone...including our parents and in-laws.

Next let's consider our siblings. Our relationships with sisters and brothers, with other in-laws, and with extended family are still relationships with family that must be lovingly, willfully, and thoughtfully nurtured and cultivated. Don't worry so much about whether or not you hold the same beliefs or see eye-to-eye on every issue. Instead, spend time in prayer for each one, asking God to show you the how's of love. You'll find (once again) that the more you pray for family members and bring them—and your heart—before God's throne of grace, the more you'll care about them and desire to be involved in their lives. And you'll find (once again) that if you spend the "treasure" of your time and emotion in prayer for these dear souls, your heart will come along (Matthew 6:21).

I can't resist a word about nieces and nephews. Wow! What an impact you as a godly aunt can have on these added blessings in your life! Imagine…spending your life loving and praying for these boys and girls…who grow up to have their own little boys and girls! I love every opportunity I have to autograph my children's books[1] for a compassionate aunt to give to her niece or nephew. Beloved sister, this is how God meant for the family to be—important, vital, a passion and a pursuit. There should be a fierceness when it comes to family—any person in our family. After all, they are our lifeblood, our blood kin…and we have a responsibility to care—and to care deeply—for and about them. Not to do so would be unnatural.

Take an inventory. Is there any one family member whom you are failing to love, to put forth the effort to care for, to pray for? I know there are those in every family who may be more difficult. I understand that things happen over the years in family relationships. But to be whole, to be blameless, to be what *we* need to be before God—women who desire to live our lives according to God's guidelines— we must make the effort, look to the Lord for help, and set the goal to improve any struggling relationships. Don't give up on being a friend to family!

Now, precious sister, how are *your* family relationships? Do they take top billing in your heart—and on your busy schedule? Are they glorifying to God? Are family members the priority people in your life? And do your daily efforts and plans and calendar reflect a commitment on your part to manage them as such?

Friendships Within the Family of God

After physical family comes the family of God. Christians are members of the family of God, heirs of God, and joint heirs with Christ (Romans 8:14-17). Therefore, believers are brothers and sisters in Christ. This means you and I have a tremendous responsibility to the family of God. And I strongly believe our best friends should be Christians, believers who pull us along and pull us up toward Christlikeness. Our best friends should be our soul partners. They should be strong, like-minded Christians who help us to think our best thoughts, do our noblest deeds, and be our finest selves.

That's what the two Old Testament friends Jonathan and David were to one another. They were soul partners. They were, as the great philosopher Aristotle defined friendship, "a single soul dwelling in two bodies."[2] What was it that made their friendship a guide for us? What did they have in common that so knit their hearts and souls together? What was the recipe that set up their friendship as God's model for all?

Love for the Lord—Prior to meeting, Jonathan and David each possessed a soul and a heart that burned and lived for one thing and one thing only—the Lord. The passion and purpose of each of these men's lives was God—living for God, serving God, pleasing God, being used of God, and extolling God. Then, the split second they met, their God-centered hearts were knit together. As one has well observed,

> Great souls by instinct to each other turn,
> demand alliance, and in friendship burn.[3]

When David's great soul faced up to Goliath, and Jonathan's great soul saw and heard David fell the giant "in the name of the LORD of hosts, the God of the armies of Israel" (1 Samuel 17:45), Jonathan instantly loved David as his own soul, and vice versa. Thus a friendship was born. Why? Because both men viewed life from a God-perspective. They…

> assented to the same authority,
> knew the same God,
> were going the same way,
> longed for the same things,
> dreamed mutual dreams,
> yearned for the same experiences
>   of holiness and worship.[4]

Love for one another—How was their brotherly love expressed? How did Jonathan and David live out their friendship?

✓ They desired the best for each other. There was no jealousy of the position, success, or accomplishments of the other. Instead, Jonathan and David followed the Bible's ideal that we rejoice with those who rejoice (Romans 12:15) and with those who are honored (1 Corinthians 12:26). They sought and supported…and delighted in…the best for each other.

✓ They encouraged the best in each other. How did Jonathan and David do this? They "strengthened" one another "in God" (1 Samuel 23:16). They pulled each other along spiritually and they pulled each other up in, and toward, the Lord. That's one of the measure of true friendship, for "insomuch as any one pushes you nearer to God, he or she is your friend."[5]

✓ They gave their best to each other. When loyalty was called for, loyalty was given. When protection was needed, protection was given. When assurance was required, assurance was given. When correction was crucial, correction was given. Through time spent together, prayer for one another, words of exhortation shared, and mutual worship, Jonathan and David gave their best to each other.

Now, dear one, who do you spend the bulk of your time with? Are your closest friends from within the family of God? Are they facing with you in the same direction— toward a common Lord? Are they soul partners who also aim toward God's highest standards?

Jonathan and David were *soul partners*.

But there's another kind of partnership in the family of God, and that is *ministry partners*. When you and someone else minister together, a deep-level friendship is born. Whether you serve on a committee, set up or clean up for events, visit convalescent homes together, or serve together in the jail ministry, your bond will be firm. That's what happened to Paul and Timothy and Silas. They loved and served the same God and were inseparable as friends.

And that's what happened in the ministry my husband pastored. As pastor of evangelism, his assignment in our church was to organize and train teams to go out on visitation and share the gospel of Jesus Christ with others. The group spent intense time in Scripture memory and preparation. Then before each team left the church, there was an intense time of prayer for open doors and open hearts. I'm sure you're not surprised to learn that lasting friendships were formed between team members and among the group. Why? Because of mutual ministry. They were involved in the throes of ministry, in spiritual work, and, linking arms together, they fought in battle side-by-side and shoulder-to-shoulder.

Their friendships were not founded on marital or work status or on their age—or the ages of their children. No, they were established on service to God, on prayer together, on the study of God's Word, and on a spiritual cause. Once you've tasted a friendship formed with a ministry partner, you'll want that element in all your friendships...as well you should!

Soul partners and ministry partners. What a blessing! And the church is filled with other partners—with the many saints that make up the body of Christ. And you and I have a responsibility to befriend and serve them, too. We'll spend some delightful time in our "ministry" chapters regarding our time and our relationships with those in the church. But for now, just remember—we are to love one another (John 13:34) and stimulate one another to love and good works (Hebrews 10:24).

Friendships Outside the Church

We all have acquaintances—neighbors, fellow workers, people we regularly encounter outside of church. But do you realize that, as you and I form friendships with each and every one of these dear souls, in every encounter...

> ...Christ is seen through our love,
> ...the seed of the gospel is sown and
> watered, and
> ...a soul is touched with the goodness of
> God?

As we nurture these casual acquaintances, there should never be any doubt about our relationship with God through

Jesus Christ. We are not "secret agents." No, coupled with our friendliness and genuine concern and caring actions, we are to be bold and outspoken about our faith in Christ. And we should faithfully and earnestly pray for the opportunity to introduce these friends to our Savior. We have no greater gift to give them than the knowledge of salvation through Jesus Christ! That's what Paul desired. He prayed in Colossians 4:3-6, for himself and for all believers, to this effect:

> that God would open a door for the word,
> to speak the mystery of Christ and declare
>   it openly,
> to walk in wisdom toward non-Christians,
> to make the most of every moment of
>   opportunity,
> for speech that is gracious and seasoned
>   with salt,
> to know how to answer any questions.

There's more to come on cultivating friendships. But for now, make Paul's prayer your own and determine to not only *reach out* to those around you, but to also *speak out!*

Looking at Life

Dear friend, one of the key ingredients of life is people...and people take time. So do friendships. As I recall again the busy day detailed at the beginning of this chapter, I want to tell you that it was *wondrously* busy! Each and every person who crossed my path that day was a friend sent by God and represented a part of His purpose for my day and my life. And each and every one of them was a soul, a needy soul, needy for something. For many what was required was simply a big smile and a hearty hello. For others it was a touch, a hug, a kind word. For one or two it was a sunshine call just to cheer and encourage. For another it was a listening heart and a prayer over the phone. And for the college women...well, their van was caught in a swollen river, causing them to arrive soaking wet two hours late. For them it was dry pajama bottoms and sweats to wear (while we put their clothes through the dryer), a hot bowl of chili, and a fire in the fireplace.

You and I must manage our time and our lives, our projects and our priorities. And we'll get to the how-to's. We'll find the balance. But the social area of our life has to do with *people*. With *souls*. And our calling first and foremost is to be a friend to all. Why, our Jesus was the Friend of sinners (Matthew 11:19) and is our Friend who sticks closer than a brother (Proverbs 18:24).

If we are truly interested in living a life of passion and purpose, then we'll have to admit that one of our purposes is to be the friend of all. Therefore, we *must* nurture and manage all our friendships—

- our *communal* friendships—with husband, children, and family,
- our *consistent* friendships—with best friends,
- our *casual* friendships—with acquaintances, and
- our *"coincidental"* friendships—with strangers.

Chapter 13

Ten Disciplines
for Managing Your Friendships

Do not forsake your own friend.
—PROVERBS 27:10

In our day of fences, block walls, property dividers, gated communities, secure highrises and condos, it's easy to find yourself "walled off" from people. Add to these barricades telephone answering machines, blocked-call devices, and voice mail, and the chances of friendships and interesting encounters with people get even slimmer. Yet friendships are a part of God's plan and a major means of mutual growth, encouragement, stimulation, learning, and love... not to mention witnessing and evangelism. Biblical friendships definitely bless us and build us up.

The Bible provides a rich photo album of precious friendships for us to examine, appreciate, and copy. From the Old Testament and New Testament alike you and I can view friendships between the saints. For instance,

David, as we've already seen, had his Jonathan...and vice versa (1 Samuel 18-20).

161

King Saul had his loyal men, who risked their lives to remove his and his sons' bodies from their execution site (1 Samuel 31).

Elijah had his faithful Elisha, who refused to leave his side (2 Kings 2).

Jesus had Joseph of Arimathea, who risked his life to recover Jesus' body after His disciples fled (Luke 23 and John 19).

Paul had Priscilla and Aquila, his helpers in Christ who risked their necks for Paul (Romans 16).

Paul had friends who wept at the thought of his potential peril (Acts 13).

Paul also had Titus (2 Corinthians 2) and Onesiphorus (2 Timothy 1).

From these examples—and more—you and I can learn many of the scriptural disciplines and habits that create and define friendships. Take the disciplines that follow to heart, and put them to work for you as you seek to be a better friend to all. As we move through this list, keep in mind that all the disciplines apply to your relationships with those in your family, those in the family of God, and all other friendships.

1.   Be loyal.

Mark it well—the most endearing...and enduring... quality between two friends is loyalty! As a tongue-in-cheek

162

English proverb declares, "God save me from my friends; I can take care of my enemies."

In the last chapter we witnessed and inspected the wonderful qualities that marked the friendship between David and Jonathan. Now, *there* was a friendship between two parties who were equally loyal! Jonathan's loyalty extended to standing up to his own father, King Saul, in defense of David. And David's loyalty extended into the next generation when he fulfilled his promise to Jonathan to take care of his family. These two soul-partners lived out the principle taught in Proverbs 18:24—"There is a friend who sticks closer than a brother." Such is the mark of loyalty.

Unfortunately, David also teaches us about the anguish caused by the *dis*-loyalty of friends. In Psalm 41 David pours out his heart to the Lord about his enemies. Sadly, he reports that "even my own familiar *friend* in whom I trusted, who ate my bread, has lifted up his heel against me" (verse 9). One translation of this verse refers to the traitor as David's "bosom friend," reporting that his "*closest* and *most trusted* friend" had turned on him.[1] Hear David's pathos in this passage—"For it is not an enemy who reproaches me; then I could bear it. Nor is it one who hates me....But it was you, a man my equal, my companion and my acquaintance. We took sweet counsel together, and walked to the house of God" together (Psalm 55:12-14). We can't help but think of the ultimate betrayal, that of Jesus by Judas, one of Jesus' own, one of His twelve disciples, one whom He called "friend" (Matthew 26:50)!

Everyone's been burned by a turncoat friend or two. Unfortunately, even in churches and between Christians, those we trust most can betray us. For whatever reasons, it does happen. But the most important thing in your friendships is that *you* be loyal. You cannot be responsible for the other person's behavior. But you are responsible for yours. Make sure *you* follow these guidelines for loyalty in friend-ships—

> Allegiance—"Do not forsake your own friend" (Proverbs 27:10),
> Devotion—"A friend loves at all times, and a brother is born for adversity" (Proverbs 17:17), and
> Silence—"He who repeats a matter separates the best of friends" (Proverbs 17:9).

Dear friend, a true soul stands by its friend...no matter what is going on. Oh, at times there may need to be correction and hearty counsel. That's a part of true friendship too—"Faithful are the wounds of a friend" (Proverbs 27:6). But there is no desertion. As an award-winning definition of a friend tells it, "A friend is the one who comes in when the whole world has gone out."² In short, stay true, stay faithful, and stay quiet!

2. Do not keep score.

I'll never forget the day I discovered the true meaning of one of the verses in the Bible's "love" chapter, 1 Corinthians 13. I had read it many times—love "thinks no evil" (verse 5). And I thought I knew what it meant. But underneath these seemingly understandable words is a surprising message. Love "thinks no evil" means love "never reckons up her wrongs, keeps no score of wrongs, does not keep account of evil."³ Love does not keep track of wrongs. Sometimes I hear a mother say to a child, "You've done that twice now. If you do it a third time, I'm going to do such and such to you."

This may be a way of disciplining and training a child, but it's *not* the way of friendship. True friends *don't* keep accounts or keep score of wrongs or failures or offenses. True friends *don't* count to three, or to ten! True friends *don't* say, "I'll give you three wrongs" or "ten wrongs" and then you're off my list. No, true friends are friends…period.

And not only does love not keep score of wrongs, but love doesn't keep score of anything! Have you ever heard someone say something like this—"The Smiths had us over for dinner. Now we need to pay them back," or "We had the Smiths over for dinner. I wonder why they haven't invited us to their house"? I know that many people consider "payback" a standard practice of hospitality, even an obligation. But true friends don't keep track.

True friends also don't get upset when a birthday is forgotten. True friends don't pay attention to whether or not you return their phone calls every time or immediately. True friends aren't shaken when time passes and there is no contact. There are no wrong or impure or selfish motives in true friendships. There is no accounting, no record-keeping, no game-playing (and keeping score), no tit-for-tat. True friends don't care if you don't get a chance to talk or speak at church, if you don't sit together at events or Bible study, if you spend time with someone else, if you are a part of other groups.

Instead friends—*true* friends—understand and support your commitments and your responsibilities and your priorities (and your busy life). They even help you with them. They are thrilled and pleased when you succeed, when you serve the Lord and His people. They rejoice (1 Corinthians 12:26) when you are honored, when you achieve some important milestone, when you do well in your undertakings. And they understand the time that living out God's plan and purposes and your stewardship and your spiritual giftedness and your priorities takes. They delight in praying for you, in encouraging you, in assisting you as you live for God and for others.

As one has well said, "Friendship is as God, who gives and asks no payment."[4] Be sure you do as Jesus said to do (and did)—be sure you give...expecting nothing in return (Luke 6:35).

3.   Be respectful and sensitive.

One way to be respectful is to be scarce. There are a multitude of ways friends can communicate without having to be together physically. We have the phone, e-mail, even the postal services...and prayer! As the proverbs teach us, "Seldom set foot in your neighbor's house, lest he become weary of you and hate you" (Proverbs 25:17), and "He who blesses his friend with a loud voice, rising early in the morning, it will be counted a curse to him" (Proverbs 27:14).

Here's how my friends and I approach each other. When we call on the phone we always ask, "Is this a good time to talk? Is everyone gone (kids to school, husband to work)?" And if it's not a good time, then we say, "I'll call back later," or "Call me when it's convenient for you."

We also call before we stop by or drop in. There are no surprises. As I said above, everyone has their goals, projects, responsibilities, ministries, preparations for the family and the home. We all have our families to serve, our housework to take care of, our devotions to tend to, our ministries to prepare for. And, as I said, we respect and support these undertakings, even helping out when and where we can... even if that means being scarce!

4. Be honest…and be attentive.

The first rule in friendships is *No Flattery Allowed!* The Bible says that "a man who flatters his neighbor spreads a net for his feet" (Proverbs 29:5). Flattery has it's roots in selfishness—it wants something! Instead of speaking empty flattery, we as Christian women can compliment one another. That means we make it a point to remark on something that is true about the other. We are to purposefully mention some evidence we've noticed of a friend's character, nobility, courage, effort, change, and/or growth. It's sort of like being a spiritual cheerleader. We're saying, "Good job! Look what you did! Way to go! Keep up the good work! Keep on keeping on! You're setting a good example for me and everyone else!"

One of the richest blessings of a solid friendship is honesty. The Bible says it this way—"Faithful are the wounds of a friend," and "the sweetness of a friend" is realized "by hearty counsel" (Proverbs 27:6,9). Many will be critical of you, but few will be honest. Remember, if (like David and Jonathan) you and your friends are committed to pulling each other up and pulling each other along as you strive together to grow in godliness and in your walk with God, you will always seek to provoke, exhort, stimulate, and stir up one another to "love and good works" (Hebrews 10:24-25). True friendship calls for truth. It demands, as the title of a book puts it, *Caring Enough to Confront.*

Honesty is the giving end of friendship. But there must also be the receiving end—when we receive a friend's honest exhortation, we must be attentive. Pride tempts us to dismiss or resent what is probably painstakingly and prayerfully shared. If we don't listen, growth can be stymied. Change can be hindered. Spiritual development can be postponed.

Even if someone shares with you for the wrong reasons and in the wrong way, listen! And afterwards take the issue to God in prayer. Ask Him to reveal any kernels of truth in what was spoken. Then make the changes or follow through on the advice...and thank your friend! Thank her for caring enough to help you to grow in Christlikeness, to correct some blind spot in your conduct or your relationships.

Friendship is a two-way street—we speak the truth in love (Ephesians 4:15), and we pay attention when others speak the truth in love.

5.   Be careful with the opposite sex.

There is to be no jealousy in friendships...except in your friendship with your husband! Let's allow author and discipler Anne Ortlund to explain. She wrote these thought-provoking words about the husband/wife relationship: "Pray for more...jealousy!....The opposite of holy jealousy is indifference. It's not caring who makes a pass at your spouse; it's being good-natured and understanding over extra little flirtations; it's tolerance when two couples get too bold, too close with each other, and the words and actions get risque in the name of friendship; it's being broadminded about unfaithfulness....There must be an invisible barrier around the two of you, holding you together, that no one else can ever invade."[5]

6.   Seek to witness in your encounters.

We all have what many call "chance" acquaintances or "coincidental" encounters with strangers. But you and I both know that there is no such thing as coincidental or chance meetings. As a child of God, we know that all such meetings are providential because God arranges them.

And when such an encounter happens, we can have at least three ministries to the person who crosses our path...even for a few seconds.

- *The ministry of friendliness.* Whenever I pass by another person, I always think of Jesus who was "the friend of sinners" (Matthew 11:19) and who "went about doing good" (Acts 10:38). So I ask my heart, "What can I give this person? A smile (and I mean a *big* smile)? A hearty hello?" You and I can both minister friendliness in these simple ways. (And make sure your face, eyes, and voice "light up" when you smile and speak.)

- *The ministry of encouragement.* This ministry should go out to everyone you actually come alongside, even if it's only for a minute. Again, ask your heart, "What can I give this person? A word of encouragement? A listening ear? A comforting touch?" (And, of course, that's *with* the big smile and hearty *hello*.)

  For instance, I was attending a Christian women's event in a hotel. As I entered the ladies room, an attendant was cleaning the restroom. First the smile...then the greeting...and then I said, "Thank you for all you do to make this place so nice. It looks fabulous!" Yes, she was a stranger. And no, I'll probably never see her again in my life. But that shouldn't stop you and me from the sweet, uplifting ministry of encouraging others. Who knows what's going on in another person's life? Who knows the sadness, the hardships, the drudgery, the pain, the emptiness that may be there? And who knows…perhaps God is using you to give someone the only kind word they will receive in a 24-hour day.

• *The ministry of witnessing.* When God gives you more than a passing moment and more than a minute with another person, then you may have the opportunity to extend the ministry of witnessing. These people that you are actually with long enough to chat with can appear in elevators, in a waiting room, in a checkout line, at the park's jungle gym, on a bus, in a plane, at a ball game. When God arranges for you to have time with someone, then make it a point to use that time to be friendly, to encourage, *and* to speak of the Lord. Pray…and then open your mouth and share something that indicates your relationship with God. Sometimes nothing happens…and sometimes everything happens! But be assured that you have sown the seed of the gospel and perhaps watered the seed sown by others. Then pray to God to give the increase (1 Corinthians 3:7-8).

Jim and I have had some wonderful encounters with fellow travelers on trips. And many times our "chance" meetings grow into the exchange of addresses. I always send these new "friends" of ours an autographed book, a little personal note, and a pamphlet that shares the Good News of Jesus Christ. And if they have little ones at home or grandchildren, I send along a book for the little people too. What a joy to minister to these strangers God sends along. Why, some of these strangers have become long-distance friends and pen pals! How did it happen? All because of a decision to reach out and be sensitive to the needs of others.

7. Be an incessant encourager.

Do you remember the beautiful details of the friendship between David and Jonathan? More specifically, do you remember that the Bible says that Jonathan "strengthened" David "in God" (1 Samuel 23:16)?

Well, here's what others do that encourages me. I'm encouraged when...

> ...someone lets me know they are praying for me. In fact, a dear "best friend" just sent me what she called "a prayer angel." Her note said that the little three-inch kneeling angel was meant to sit on my desk so that each day when I saw it, I would know one person was praying for me every day! Now, that's encouraging!

> ...someone sends a little note of appreciation...for no reason at all. One day a tiny "Pooh Bear" card arrived in the mail, cut in the shape of that round, cuddly bear. Inside the woman had written these words— "Dear Elizabeth, You have been so helpful/a life-saver to me. You are to me a Titus 2 woman. Thank you and may God bless you and your beautiful family and ministry—Remember, in Hebrews 6:10: 'For *God* is not unfair. *He* will not forget how hard you have worked for Him and how you have shown your love to Him by caring for other Christians (like me), as you still do.'" And the woman signed off with "Love you xxx" and her name.

Friend, I have to say, first of all, that card arrived when my heart was so far down I wondered if it would ever get "up" again! And second, these several years later, I still carry it in my personal journal that goes with me everywhere. Would you believe... hardly a day goes by that I don't read it so that the Scripture verse and this woman's love can refresh me once again? Talk about encouragement! And I've never even met the dear saint God moved to send it!

...someone is specific in their praise. When you want to praise and encourage someone, be sure you are specific. Don't be general—"Hey, that was great." And don't be ordinary—"I sure do thank the Lord for you." Take a few extra seconds to be specific. "I always appreciate the way you..." "I was watching you minister to that elderly woman, and you taught me a large lesson by the way you..."

I'm sure you can add to my list. But do be an incessant encourager. My precious Jim is a true people-person. And he taught me his principle for his encounters with others—"In every encounter make it your goal that the other person is better off for having been in your presence." I'm happy to admit, this people principle has become mine, too, and I hope will become yours as well.

8. Prioritize your friendships.

You only have so much time in a day and in a life. So it's vitally important that you identify whom you are spending the bulk of your time with. Is it your family? Your best friends? Christians? Is it those who pull you up and pull you along in your spiritual growth and walk with God? Is it those who help you to live out God's plan for your life with excellence? Who help you seek to set your affection on things above? Or is your time mostly spent with the girls at work? Unbelievers? A nearby neighbor? There's nothing wrong with giving of yourself to these acquaintances. But be sure they are not eating away your time…the time you could be studying the Word, being in a Bible study, being discipled, or being involved in a ministry. And be sure you are reaching out and ministering to these wonderful acquaintances at work, etc. The best thing you can do for these friends is to find out (that means listening!) the details of their lives, let them know how much you care for them and that you are praying for them, and continually ask them to come along with you to church or to your Bible study. Better yet, ask them to get together and have a Bible study with you!

9. Nurture your friendships.

We never wake up in the morning and coldheartedly, calculatingly decide, "I think I'll neglect my friends today." No, the neglect is most subtle. We just wake up in the morning and don't even *think* about our friends! Therefore, our friendships must be nurtured. You and I have to make willful decisions about the maintenance and growth of friendships—with both family and friends. And that takes time, care, and love. It takes some money, too, as we purchase little cards, small gifts, something that shouts out that person's name when we walk by, something she collects, uses, loves, enjoys, reads, appreciates. It may take even more money as we travel long distances to sustain our precious friendships with individuals or other couples.

173

Here are a few things I do to nurture friendships. First, I make sure my friends receive autographed, inscribed copies of every book I write...right out of the first case off the press. (And, just to set the record straight, my two daughters receive the first two books out of the first box off the press!) Then, whatever store I'm in for whatever reason, I purposefully look for things my family and friends like, that fit into their lifestyles or houses, or that advance their personal goals. Also, because I'm a catalog shopper (after all, we do live in the country!), I keep a list of items I see in my catalogs that would be terrific Valentine's Day, Easter, birthday, Mother's Day, Thanksgiving, or Christmas gifts. These items are usually small and inexpensive. But about once every month or two, I absolutely delight in sending "a little something" to my friends.

As Paul said of his friends in Philippi, "I have you in my heart" (Philippians 1:7). As you nurture your friendships day after day, you will find that you do truly carry them in your heart. I even find that I *am* my friends! It's hard to explain, but because of the time spent with them, the time spent thinking about them and caring and praying for them, their influence and "nearness in heart" becomes a part of my life. And this is a good thing, because they are the ones who are pulling me up and pulling me along in Christlikeness and in my spiritual growth. We become like twin sisters in Christ, never far from one another in heart.

10. Pray for your friends.

Dear one, we have no greater or finer (or more costly!) gift to give both our family and friends than to pray for them—faithfully, frequently, and fervently. Everyone struggles, and everyone faces trials and encounters crises. And we can be sure there are issues in our friends' lives that will never be shared with us. We'll never know all the battles that are being fought in another person's life. So we pray.

Pray, dear one, for your friends' spiritual growth, for their marriage, for their ministry, for their work on the job, for others to come along and encourage them too. And share with them exactly what you are praying. Pass on the specific scriptures you use as you beseech God on their behalf. You never know when the Bible verse you share just might be the perfect "word in season" that strengthens your weary friend (Isaiah 50:4) and helps her to get through a tough day. And you never know when *you* just might be the true friend whose faithful, frequent, and fervent prayers help another to excel in greatness...or make it through a difficult life!

Looking at Life

Yes, dear friend (for that's what I desire to be to you), God intended us to have friends and to be a friend. We are social beings. We long to love and to be loved. That's the way God made us. So I want to encourage you in all your relationships—be the best friend anyone could ever have!

But I also want to caution you that friendships—true friendships—come with a price tag. And that price tag includes *time!* I'm praying as I write that I can make this clear. This book is about time and life management. This book is about managing our time so that our lives are complete and balanced, with no major areas of life omitted or neglected...or indulged!

So when it comes to living out God's plan for your time and your life, you must realize that friendships *take* time. And friendships *require* time. Therefore, beloved, you will not be able to have an abundance of friends. There just isn't time to nurture a multitude of friendships. If you're like me, your days are already full of the work your responsibilities demand. And if you're like me, your days aren't even long enough to *do* the work your responsibilities demand. So choose wisely. *Be* the best friend you can be to everyone... but *choose* wisely who your best friends will be. And how will you recognize those friends?

> A real friend
> is one who helps us to
> think our best thoughts,
> do our noblest deeds, and
> be our finest selves.[6]

Ten Commandments of Friendship

1. Speak to people—there is nothing as nice as a cheerful word of greeting.

2. Smile at people—it takes seventy-two muscles to frown and only fourteen to smile!

3. Call people by name—the sweetest music to anyone's ear is the sound of their own name.

4. Be friendly and helpful—if you would have friends, be friendly.

5. Be cordial—speak and act as if everything you do were a real pleasure.

6. Be genuinely interested in people—you can like *everyone* if you try.

7. Be generous with praise—cautious with criticism.

8. Be considerate of the feelings of others—it will be appreciated.

9. Be thoughtful of the opinions of others.

10. Be alert to give service—what counts most in life is what we do for others![7]

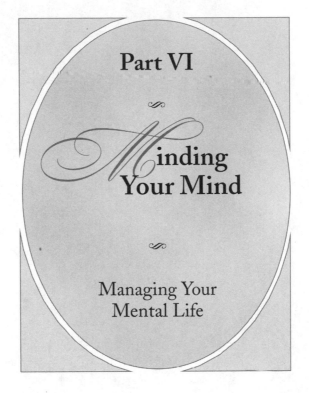

Part VI

Minding
Your Mind

Managing Your
Mental Life

Chapter 14

God's Guidelines
for Your Mind

Finally, brethren, whatever things are true...noble...just...
pure...lovely...of good report, if there is any virtue and...
anything praiseworthy—[think] on these things.
—PHILIPPIANS 4:8

"Managing Your Mental Life." I have to admit, I just chuckled as I typed these words on the previous page! Images and clichés of a "mental breakdown" and being "a mental case" just came to "mind." Hopefully neither image will become a reality for you or me!

Dodging mental breakdowns and successfully avoiding becoming a mental case is *not* what this section of our book is about. What it *is* about is our thought life, about what we choose to think about, about what we choose to put into our minds, about how we choose to use the 12 to 14 billion cells that make up our brains. It's about minding our minds. In order to live out God's plan for our lives in the midst of great busy-ness and live it out with passion and purpose, we must harness the 10,000-plus thoughts that supposedly pass through our minds each day. And we must direct and discipline the use of the world's most powerful computer—our brain—so it is used for God's purposes and for His glory.

That's a tall challenge, isn't it? But thankfully the Bible gives us clear directions and guidelines for mastering and managing the mental area of our lives and the use of our minds...for Him.

God's Guidelines: What to Think...and Not Think

Our minds are active, constantly bringing things to our consciousness, things that we can then choose to think on or not think on. So obviously it helps us in managing our mental life to know the standards God sets for our choices about what we think or don't think. One very specific set of standards is given to us in Philippians 4:8. Here Paul writes, "Finally, brethren, whatever things are true, whatever things are noble, whatever things are just, whatever things are pure, whatever things are lovely, whatever things are of good report, if there is any virtue and if there is anything praiseworthy—meditate on these things," or "think on these things" (KJV).

Did you notice the command at the end of this verse—"think on these things"? What things? Things that are true, noble, just, pure, lovely, of good report, virtuous, and praiseworthy. This is a checklist from God for evaluating our thoughts. And asking the following questions about our thoughts helps you and me line up our thoughts with God's requirements. (Plus it brings forth a bouquet of blessings as we think godly thoughts!)

✓ *Is it true?*—Or is what I'm thinking a lie, a rumor, a suspicion? Am I entertaining facts...or hearsay...or speculation? Am I second-guessing or reading between the lines? And most importantly, is what I'm thinking true to God's character and His Word?

✓ *Is it noble?*—Is this thought dignified and excellent? Is it my best, highest thought? Or is it shoddy, second-rate, cheap, beneath the dignity that should characterize everything about my life as a Christian...including this thought? Is it sacred, or is it profane? Is it unworthy of me as God's child and of the person it's aimed at? Better yet, does it have the decency and dignity of holiness upon it?

✓ *Is it just?*—Is this a right and righteous thought, lining up with the regulations of God's truth? Is this thought in harmony with God's divine standard of holiness? Is it encouraging me to do what is right toward my fellow man, to follow through on my duties and responsibilities, to live up to God's Word and His guidelines for my life?

✓ *Is it pure?*—Is what I'm thinking holy, spotless, wholesome, completely without sin? Could this thought be brought into the presence of God?

✓ *Is it lovely?*—Is this a thought of 100 percent moral and spiritual beauty, or is it tainted with vileness and evil? Is it gracious? Is it set on that which is kind and forbearing, or is it critical and harmful?

✓ *Is it of good report?*—If someone else were privy to this thought, would that person think it was commendable? Would it speak well of me and of the one thought about? Is this thought worthy of being contemplated, let alone of being verbalized? Is it kind and gracious, high-toned, and directed at the fine, good things in others?

✓ *Is it praiseworthy?*—Would this thought merit the praise of others? Of God? If this thought were verbalized, would it pass the test of the Bible's guidelines? Would it meet with God's approval?

✓ *Is there any virtue?*—Is this vein of thinking filled with all moral excellence? Will it motivate me to live a better life for Christ?

As I said, you and I can (and must!) use these eight questions and qualities as a checklist for our thoughts. If they pass the test, then, as Paul said, we can think on these things. These are the kinds of rich, uplifting, godly thoughts that we are to treasure in our heart, to dwell on, and to cherish. As one Bible translation bids us, "let such be your treasures." Think and meditate and dwell on...and treasure *these* things!

Now, here's a "thought." What thoughts can we be sure meet God's standards? What do we *know* fits the bill for the "things" we are told in Scripture to think on? The answer? God, God's Son, and God's Word. To be safe—and blessed... and transformed (Romans 12:2)—just think about Deity and dwell on God's Word. Beloved, think on *these* things!

Our thoughts should be like an evergreen—Here in the Pacific Northwest, where Jim and I now live, there are glorious evergreen trees everywhere! In fact, out my kitchen window is what I call "the cathedral." (Actually, I think of it as *my* cathedral!) It's a mountainside of forest. And the firs, cedars, and pines that pack its slope are characterized by one thing (other than being green)—everything about the trees points upward. The evergreens' trunks shoot up, straight as arrows, into the sky. Even all of the limbs on the trees and their twiggy growth stretch and bow and bend upward. Every visible part of these trees is reaching, striving, and pushing upward, sunward, heavenward, Godward!

And, dear one, our thoughts should be like those evergreens. They should reach ever upward. That's what the scripture in Philippians 4:8 calls us to. Notice well the Bible's choice of words—"true...noble...just...pure...lovely...good ...virtuous...praiseworthy." Don't just skip, scan, and speed over these precious jewels. No, read them again! Behold them. Savor them. Say them out loud. Let their goodness and grandeur roll through your mouth and your mind...and your soul. This is heavenly language. And God calls—and commands—us to think heavenly, godly thoughts.

Our thoughts should be like a cathedral—Maybe my reflection on a "cathedral" fits here as well. Think of yourself as entertaining thoughts in the cathedral of your mind. Think of them as being like the strong stone pillars inside a grand cathedral that run upward, losing themselves in the loftiness of a cathedral's upper limits. See that they are your best thoughts. That they're guileless thoughts. Think the thoughts that speak the best of you, of God, and of others. Think thoughts that measure high on the scale of the size and greatness of a cathedral. As preacher-of-old D. L. Moody shares, "If we look down, then our shoulders stoop. If our thoughts look down, our character bends. It is only when we hold our heads up that the body becomes erect. It is only when our thoughts go up that our life becomes erect."[1]

Our thoughts should be disciplined—Here's something a little more elementary than the architectural wonder of a cathedral. When my two daughters were attending the preschool and primary departments in our church's Sunday school, they learned a song that tells even you and me what to do and not do when it comes to our thoughts and the use of our minds. One stanza of the song warns, "Be careful, little mind, what you think." Doesn't that about say it all? As women who desire to live out God's plan and purpose for our lives we've got to be careful what we think! As a well-used saying teaches,

> Sow a thought, reap an action.
> Sow an action, reap a habit.
> Sow a habit, reap a character.
> Sow a character, reap a destiny![2]

Our actions, habits, character, and future are most definitely affected by our thoughts. So you and I as women with a passion for God and godly thoughts must be careful and disciplined when it comes to our thoughts. We must be willful about what we think and don't (and *won't!*) think. We must do as the Bible teaches and "*seek* those things which are above" and "*set* [our] mind on things above, not on things on the earth" (Colossians 3:1-2). We must make sure our thoughts are ever aimed and ascending upward so that our character is ever arching upward and our lives are upright.

What to Do...and Not Do

Isn't it nice to know that God has given us some curbs for our thought life? It's so liberating to know what His boundaries are regarding what we are to think...and not think.

But there is another side to our minds—the mental energy involved in determining what we do...and don't do. Here are a few of the mental activities that direct our lives so that we purposefully live out God's plan. These exercises will help you determine what to do...and not to do with your time and your life.

Problem solving—When we set our minds and thoughts to good, better, and best use, we can enlist its help in problem solving. As we think about God's plan and the directions for life and for the priorities He gives us in His Word, we can settle on His solution to our problems.

Decision making—Not a second goes by that you and I aren't making decisions. As you listen to someone speak, you have to carefully decide how to answer...and with what words. When there is a crisis, options have to be clicked through mentally on the spot...and a decision on a course of action must be made quickly. And when there is a lull in the action—a surprising pause in the midst of your busy life or day, a sudden quiet moment in the whirlwind of life—well, beware! We must decide how to put those moments to use. We can give in to laziness, self-indulgence, or to secondary (even lower!) choices...or we can wisely decide to seize the opportunity, redeem the time (Colossians 4:5), and put it to good use. Remember, your ability to make wise decisions is directly proportional to your degree of maturity.

Planning—The first book I ever read on time management bluntly stated, "Fail to plan? Plan to fail!" Of course, all the books I've ever read on managing time and life also suggested that I spend at least 20 minutes on the front end of each day planning. And you and I both know how planning is done. It's done with the mind! We must *think!* We must think through the minutes and the hours of our day. And we must choose what to do...and not do. We must also decide on an order for our work, on the conservation of energy, on the delegation of tasks and work, on the completion of deadlines (like dinner each evening!). And this kind of planning goes on when we also consider our week, our month, our year, and our life as well.

Organizing—And don't forget organizing! To organize means to arrange in an orderly way. For instance, what order do you put things in? Things like the order of your priorities? Things like the order for your day, and what you work on, and when? Things like the order of importance regarding the tasks on your to-do list? Things like the order of the activities required to complete a task or project? Things like the order of the errands you must run...and their importance?

Recently my daughter Courtney told me that while running errands with her three preschoolers under three years old in the back seat of the car, she decided not to run the final errand so that the whole outing didn't fall apart. But she got the most important errands taken care of. Why? Because she had prioritized—organized—her errand list.

Now, that's the kind of beauty (and sanity!) organizing brings to our busy lives. But it's done with the mind...and it takes time and effort.

Scheduling—Finally, there is scheduling. If planning is determining *what* I need to do, and organizing is determining *how* I need to do it, then scheduling is determining *when* I need to do it. *When* is the best time to begin a project, go to the grocery store, work your Bible study lesson, prepare for the Sunday school class you teach? Use your mind to think through these activities that represent your unique life, to make decisions, to prioritize, and then to schedule them in a way that makes the living out of your day and your life go more smoothly.

Looking at Life

Now, about our busy-ness. I have to tell you that it was extremely difficult to decide what order to use in presenting the sections of this book and the areas of life you and I are called upon by God to live. I knew the spiritual area had to be first and foremost (…always!). We know that without God's help we can do nothing. We also know that all of the guiding principles for life—and a busy life—come to us from God's Word. And we know that in order to live our lives with passion and purpose they must be lived for and unto the Lord.

But then what? I chose to place the physical area of life second. That's because of the tremendous amount of energy—physical energy—it takes to live out God's plan for our lives. We have a lot to do—for *Him* and for *them* (those in the family, the church, and others).

But, dear one, I could have just as easily placed the mental area of life second. Why? Because of how greatly our thoughts impact our life. For instance, our thoughts can energize us…or exhaust us. They can direct us toward God's way and God's will…or they can divert us from the path of following Him. They can help us…or hinder us as we seek to live out God's plan for our lives. They can serve us as allies…or foil us as enemies.

Beloved, don't fail to use your mind! Don't fail to manage your thoughts! And don't trifle away your precious time and day…and life! Don't neglect…

...to solve your problems God's way,

...to make decisions that reflect God's purposes,

...to plan to live out God's plan for your life,

...to organize your life according to God's priorities, and

...to schedule your day so that God is glorified and the people in your life are blessed.

Hear now these words that come to us across the centuries from the passionate heart of David Brainerd, missionary and "apostle to the American Indians," a man who lived his life with passion and purpose...and who died at age 29! Let his fiery words shed light on what you are thinking...and not thinking about life; on what you are doing...and not doing with your time and your life.

> Oh, how precious is time; and how guilty it makes me feel when I think I have trifled away and misimproved it or neglected to fill up each part of it with duty to the utmost of my ability and capacity.[3]

Chapter 15

Ten Disciplines
for Managing Your Mind

And do not be conformed to this world,
but be transformed by the renewing of your mind…
—ROMANS 12:2

I just checked in my dictionary for the meaning of the word *homemaker*. Do you know what it is? A homemaker is a person who *manages* a home. For most men this six-word definition sounds like an easy assignment. Manage a home? No problem! But if you or I (or our husbands!) were to stop and really think about what's involved in home management, we (and especially our husbands!) would be shocked. More or less, you as a home manager…

> …oversee the most valuable family asset, the
> house,
> …oversee the family finances (another of the
> family's larger assets),
> …oversee the education of the children (talk about
> a responsibility!),
> …oversee the health care for the entire family,

...oversee the social calendar, and (as if that's not
enough) you also

...oversee the transportation of your darlings as
the head chauffeur.

(What a woman! Who said managing a home is easy?!)

So how does all this management take place? The answer—with your mind! Being the straw boss (a person who has subordinate authority—subordinate to God and to your husband, if you are married) requires massive mental energy and activity. It demands that we plan, organize, schedule, and execute. Just read Proverbs 31:10-31 (again) and try to grasp all the mental (not to mention physical) energy that was needed for the Proverbs 31 woman to accomplish all her tasks. It's staggering! This woman definitely had a well-trained and disciplined mind! She had definitely developed the mental capacity needed to look well to the ways of her household (Proverbs 31:27)!

Now back to us. Just how do you and I fulfill our roles as managers of not only our homes but all of life? Hopefully these next ten disciplines will help us to better manage our minds...so that we can better manage our lives.

1. Be reading your Bible.

The best way to live out God's plan for your life is to safeguard against being conformed to this world (Romans 12:2). And the surest way to guard your mind is to read your Bible. Why? Because God's Word causes you to think godly thoughts. It changes you and causes you to grow spiritually. God's Word causes you to view life and your roles and personal situations through the lens of His truth. When you read the Bible, you tune in to God's mind and receive His take and His teaching on any and every subject.

So, dear busy woman, take some of your precious time and read your precious Bible. Reading the Bible transforms and renews your mind (Romans 12:2). The Bible is a plumb line, a grid, a compass, a blueprint, and a map by which you are to live your life. Therefore reading or not reading God's Word dramatically affects your day and your life.

Ask yourself, is your focus for the day being set by exposure to the Word of God? Or is it being set by exposure to the world via television news and programs, by the morning newspaper, by talk-show hosts, by the empty chatter of workmates or classmates? Your way of thinking is transformed when you renew your mind each day (and preferably each morning!) by reading your Bible. This simple act of using your mind (and taking the time) to read your Bible changes your thinking, your perspective, your choices, your behavior, and the way you live your life. Nothing else in this world can renew our minds like the Bible, which is—

> a light to guide us,
> a rod to correct us,
> a staff to lead us,
> a mirror to reveal us,
> a banquet table to feed us, and
> a rudder to steer us.

Dear one, I can't say enough about this all-important first discipline of reading your Bible! God's Word is the tool the Holy Spirit uses to change our worldly, sensual thinking from the baser things of this world to the lofty thoughts of heaven. Only a mind that is completely immersed in the

Word of God can be truly renewed. That's why we are to be ever saturating ourselves with the Bible—so our minds are being ever renewed.

2. Be memorizing.

Do you remember our discussion of God's guidelines for our thought life in Philippians 4:8? And do you remember that Paul exhorted us to "think on these things"? I pointed out that one translation of this command paraphrases it, saying that you and I are to let such be our "treasures."

Well, treasured friend, God's Word—memorized and hidden in your heart—is a treasure no one can take away from you. One of the greatest treasures I own is the storehouse of verses I've memorized over the years. No matter where I am or what is happening in my life, no matter what the demand or the trial, I need only draw out one of my treasures, one of my jewels, one of my pearls, one of my verses from the treasure box of my heart, and I have what I need—straight from God's heart to mine. And it all started with a seminar I attended as a new Christian. And from just one sentence of the many hours of lectures given by the instructor: "You should be memorizing Scripture." As a baby Christian, I didn't yet realize that what others told me might be optional! So I dutifully and obediently went home and began memorizing Scripture! And that was 28 years ago.

Friend, you should be memorizing Scripture!

3. Be developing.

Mental growth is a progressive thing. Start where you are and develop your mental capacity.

Develop by setting goals—A goal is something you focus on that lies in the future. And goal-setting is yet another life-changing mental exercise. Jim and I wanted to develop our minds and prepare ourselves for whatever God might have in mind for us. So we sat down one Sunday afternoon and wrote out a set of lifetime goals we believed would place God, His Word, and His priorities at the center of our lives (Lord willing!). And, would you believe it, we are still following those goals to this day? How will developing a set of goals help you to better manage your busy life?

- Goals give you motivation. They keep you going when your heart or will weakens.

- Goals reflect your ideal future. As one man said, "I expect to spend the rest of my life in the future, so I want to be reasonably sure of what kind of future it's going to be."[1] (And, of course, we add, "Lord willing"!)

- Goals give you energy. The apostle Paul was energized to "reach forward" or "press on" by his goal to gain God's prize (Philippians 3:14).

- Goals give you direction. Again, Paul always knew in which direction he wanted to go. He was the man who declared, "This one thing I do..." (Philippians 3:13 KJV).

- Goals help turn your dreams into realities. King David dreamed of building a house for God. With David's plans and materials in hand, his son Solomon made the dream a reality.

- Goals are measurable. Goals are dreams with deadlines.

Develop by reading—Reading is the quickest way to develop. Reading also stimulates fresh thoughts and ideas. We've already discussed reading the Bible and being a woman of one book—the Book. Beyond the Bible, a multitude of excellent books are available for you to read. The greatest writers and theologians and teachers in the world are sharing the fruits of their decades of study. They are distilling their knowledge down…to people like you and me.

Let's take the advice of J. Oswald Sanders, author of the classic book *Spiritual Leadership*, regarding reading— "The determination to spend a minimum of half an hour a day in reading worthwhile books that provide food for the soul and further mental and spiritual development will prove richly rewarding…."[2]

Develop your professional skills—If you have a job, you represent Jesus Christ on that job. Therefore, be the best on the job. Not only is your conduct to be impeccable, but your job skills should be ever-increasing and improving.

But…just a word of caution. Your job will always be a far second to your marriage and family, your home and church. And even if you're not married, your job will always be a far second to your service in your church. You are a Christian *first*…and *then* a woman in the workforce.

In this book we're addressing living out *God's* plan for your life. And His plan for a married woman and mom is that she spend her first and best—and last!—spiritual, physical, and mental efforts on bettering the lives of her husband and children, on making a home for her family. If you also have a job, be careful to keep God's priorities written deeply and boldly on the tablet of your heart (Proverbs 3:3).

Yes, you may work at a job, but your real work, your real life, your true priorities lie at home. And they are waiting for you every day when you come home, no matter how tired you are from spending so many hours serving others. If you desire to live out God's plan for your life, then realize that His plan for you, if you are married, is first and foremost at home. He has given *you*, not someone else, the charge and care of your family and home.

You must be on guard against working all day and spending your energies at a job and then excusing yourself from the work at home. You must not be too tired from serving others *outside* the home to serve those priority people *inside* the home when you get there each evening. No, you must embrace God's priorities and flip your approach and believe—and function accordingly—that your great and grand work is at home. And you just happen to also have a job you go to. Home is where your heart must be. So whether we work or not, our hearts must be anchored at home. Our greatest passion must be our families, not our professions.

4.   Be preparing.

We never know how God will use us and our unique giftedness. But if we are prepared, there will always be opportunities. Our job is to put forth the mental energy that is required to prepare—and then look to God. God's job is to determine when we are ready. And, dear one, that will be in the fullness of *His* timing—not *ours!* But be assured, He *will* use us for His purposes and glory. After all, we are His workmanship, created in Christ Jesus for good works (Ephesians 2:10). He'll let us know what those good works are...and He'll put them on display...in His time.

5.   Be sharing.

Experts tell us that we retain 10 percent of what we hear, 40 percent of what we write down, and 60 percent of what we commit to memory. But here's the most staggering statistic of all—we retain close to 100 percent of what we teach! We may not all be teachers who stand up in front of a class, but we should all be sharing what we know. As Titus 2:3 says, you and I are called to be "teachers of good things." We are to be sharing with other women what we know about living our life according to God's plan.

So now I'm asking you, please, don't waste all the mental energy you must spend to learn something...only to file it away! When you've learned something, share it with a sister who needs what you have learned. Pass it on. That's discipleship. And it comes with a double blessing. The hearer is blessed and bettered by your knowledge. And you are blessed because you have now retained almost 100 percent of what you have learned...just because you shared it!

6.   Be challenged.

All of life's disciplines are dynamic. That means they are ever in flux, ever changing and hopefully becoming more demanding as we grow in our different areas of life. Never be satisfied with the status quo. Once you have attained a certain mental level, challenge yourself to greater heights. (And speaking of challenging yourself to greater heights, one of my favorite quotes advises, "Always aim at the moon. You may not make it, but you just might grab a star on the way by!")

7. Be varied.

The mind has an infinite capacity to absorb information. Therefore, we should use as many different avenues as we can to stimulate our thinking and expand our horizons. We've already discussed reading and memorizing. But what about listening to audiotapes? Just think, while you are slaving away over a hot iron, a hot stove, a sink full of hot water, or pounding the hot pavement on your run, you can tune in to an expert in any field of interest. Or, while you're in the car you can be listening to a master teacher rather than listening to music. And don't forget watching video-taped lectures and demonstrations.

One of the varied means I used for stretching my mind was enrolling in correspondence courses from the Moody Bible Institute Correspondence School.[3] Working these courses called for discipline upon discipline as I chose to work the lessons during my preschoolers' nap time! (And ooooh, did I ever want a nap too!) But in the end, I "graduated" from more than twenty Bible classes. Taking those courses was a goal that challenged me and caused me to develop…and prepared me for potential and future ministry that I've been now sharing with others for several decades. That's how it is when the disciplines for managing your mind are put into practice.

8. Be continuing.

Mental development is a lifelong pursuit. We've already looked at the remarkable life of J. Oswald Sanders, a man who continued to learn, grow, and share well into his nineties.

And yet so many of us think, "It's too late for me." A lady said that to me recently. After discussing our need to keep growing so that we have something to say and something to give to others in ministry, she said, "It's too late for me." (And the scary thing was that she was younger than me!)

But it's never too late! History has proven that. For instance,

> Michelangelo painted the ceiling of the Sistine Chapel on his back on a scaffold at near age 90.
> Strauss was still composing serious music after his eightieth birthday.
> Benjamin Franklin served his country in France at age 78 and wrote his autobiography at over 80.
> John Wesley, at age 83, was annoyed that he could not write more than 15 hours a day, and at 86 was ashamed that he could not preach more than twice a day.

Obviously these people never stopped using their minds and undertaking new laborious and creative challenges. And, dear one, neither should we.

9. Be reviewing.

Faithful and regular review burns truths and information into our minds. Then it becomes a part of our life. And then we can share it with others. I have three disciplines for reviewing that help keep important information fresh in my mind and my memory.

—The first is reviewing my memorized Scripture verses. They literally come alive again with each visit.

—The second is periodically reading through materials previously read, clipped, filed, and saved. A lot of vital material gets filed away, and reviewing it teaches me all over again.

—And the third is my journal. I write everything I want to remember in my journal—quotes, sermon notes, poetry, beautiful wording, advice, special dates to remember, life-changing events, ideas, dreams, goals. And I take my journal with me everywhere I go. Then, with any spare minute, I can return to the things I love most and relive them.

The end result of these three exercises is always sheer joy...but it requires the discipline of reviewing to taste that joy again and again.

Looking at Life

As I read back through the ten disciplines in this chapter, two things happened. First, I was once again challenged and motivated to keep on growing, to continue using, developing, and stretching my mind in ways that help me to live out God's will and purposes for my life. And, oh how I pray you are too! What a wonderful gift God has given us in a mind!

But second, I decided to make this final tenth discipline our heart challenge as we look once again at life. So here it is...

10.   Be selective.

Maybe it's because my mother suffers from Alzheimer's and dementia, but I am frightfully passionate about the careful, selective use of my mind. I talk to so many women and witness so many people using their minds in lesser ways that it alarms me.

So, I'll ask you, how do you use your mind? The use of your mind is a choice—*your* choice. And that's what makes it a discipline. Living out God's plan for our life requires that we discipline our choices about how we use our mind. (Imagine how drastically different a life would be if the same time and mental energy spent on lesser activities were spent instead reading the dynamic, life-changing biography of a man like David Brainerd!)

And here's another sobering truth—out of the treasure of the heart and mind, the mouth speaks (Matthew 12:34). What we put into our minds will most surely come out! So imagine instead of garbage in and garbage out, instead of trivia in and trivia out, instead of secondary things in and secondary things out, we could discipline ourselves to choose godly things in—leading to a powerful influence as godly things stream out!

It's as simple as this (and, believe me, I'm asking myself these same questions!)—Do you want to live a godly life? Then choose to put the things into your mind that lead to living a godly life. Do you want to have a better home life? Then choose to put the things into your life (the books, the classes) that lead to realizing a better home life. Do you want to have a powerful ministry? Then choose to put the things into your mind that can lead to a powerful ministry. Do you want a more balanced and orderly life? Then put the things

202

into your mind (the books, the classes) that teach your mind how to solve problems, make decisions, plan, and schedule for a more balanced and orderly life.

The point is, beloved, we must be careful! Be vigilant! Be selective! *Guard* your heart and your mind! Don't waste your mind...which is a waste of your time...which leads to a wasted life! Life is just too short and too precious to be wasted on anything that does not help you to live out God's plan and purposes for your life.

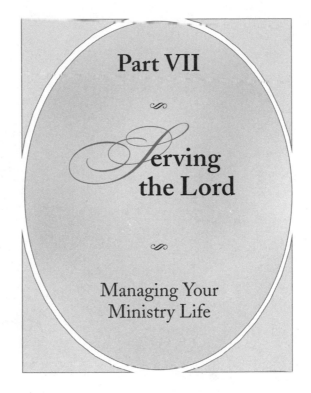

Part VII

Serving
the Lord

Managing Your
Ministry Life

Chapter 16

God's Guidelines
for Your Ministry

*Having then gifts differing according
to the grace that is given to us, let us use them.*
—ROMANS 12:6

As I interact daily with women at my church, through
the mail and e-mail, and in seminars, I'm often asked how
my teaching and writing ministry began. And I always have
to answer, "Not in a very exciting way!" No, it wasn't very
exciting at all! Sharing God's Word with women like you all
began with a letter I received—a letter to the wives of all
the pastors, elders, and deacons at my church that began
with the very warm, personal greeting of…"Dear friend."
The letter went on to solicit servers, teachers, administra-
tors, and pray-ers for the launching of a new women's ministry that was about to begin at my church.

When I read the sentence that basically asked, "Do you
have anything you might want to teach the women as an
elective workshop?" my first response was, "Not me, Lord!
I've never taught anything from the Bible. And it's just too
great a responsibility. Doesn't your Word say, 'Be not many
teachers'?"

But then, after much prayer and heart searching, there arose from my heart a second response that stemmed from a decision I had made much earlier. As a new Christian, I had made a commitment in my heart (and written out on paper) to

1. take care of my ministry to my family,

2. grow in my knowledge of the Bible,

3. develop my spiritual gifts, and

4. be willing to serve others whenever God determined I was ready.

Well, dear one, it seemed that the letter of invitation (albeit a *form* letter!) presented an obvious opportunity to attempt serving the women in my church. It seemed to live out writer and teacher Charles Swindoll's definition of success—"Success is when preparation meets opportunity." There's no doubt that God is the Bringer of opportunity! But there's also no doubt that you and I are the ones who must choose to do the preparing!

So, having gotten my act together in my family as a wife, mother, and home manager (somewhat, anyway...it is a lifelong pursuit!), I stepped out, stepped across the line, and stepped up to the challenge to see how I could serve the family of God. After all, God gives us roles and responsibilities in both families.

And so I began to seek to live out God's ministry plan for me, to live out my giftedness to serve the Lord in my church.

Our Giftedness to Serve the Lord

Did you know that every Christian is gifted by God to serve the body of Christ? That's what the Bible teaches—

- Paul teaches us that "having then gifts differing according to the grace that is given to us, let us use them" in the body of Christ (Romans 12:6).

- Paul teaches us again that "the manifestation of the Spirit is given to each one for the profit of all" (1 Corinthians 12:7).

- Paul also teaches us that "to each one of us grace was given according to the measure of Christ's gift" (Ephesians 4:7).

- Peter teaches us, too, that "as each one has received a gift, minister it to one another, as good stewards of the manifold grace of God" (1 Peter 4:10).

Therefore we could say that the first guideline for our life of ministry is to recognize that you and I as Christian women are gifted to serve the Lord. We are gifted by God through the Holy Spirit to benefit and better the body of Christ. As we learned above, "the manifestation of the Spirit is given to each one for the profit of all" (1 Corinthians 12:7). And, as we learned above, we are commanded to "use" our spiritual gifts and to "minister" to one another as good, responsible "stewards." God has entrusted us with His grace gifts, which we are to manage (that's what a steward does), develop, and use for Him.

Our Array of Service to the Lord

Here's another beautiful (and comforting!) fact and guideline about our spiritual giftedness—the gifts are varied. There is a broad array of spiritual gifts whereby believers serve the Lord and His people. True, the gifts are all given by the Holy Spirit, designated and distributed to believers as

209

God wills, and empowered by the same Spirit. But the spiritual gifts are diverse and different (1 Corinthians 12:1-11). The beauty of the gifts is in their Source and their variety...and the comfort is in the fact that the gifts are unique to each one of us. Our gift will not necessarily be like anyone else's, nor should it be. (Now, that's comforting!)

Some of the gifts—What is the array of the spiritual gifts? The major lists are found in Romans 12:6-8 and 1 Corinthians 12:8-10. And the book of 1 Peter seems to imply that spiritual gifts lie in two categories—*speaking* gifts and *serving* gifts (1 Peter 4:11).

Three of the gifts—We'll spend our whole life discovering, developing, and ministering our spiritual gifts. However, no Christian is to wait on this process before he or she begins to care for believers in their church. No, you and I are commanded to love one another fervently (1 Peter 1:22). And three of the spiritual gifts—serving, giving, and showing mercy—are also commanded of us. So, as a new Christian, I once again found a "comfort zone" (and you can too!) in these three gifts as I began to simply live out God's commands to serve, give, and show mercy.

To this day I pray each and every morning to serve anyone and everyone who comes across my path...especially those who are of the household of faith (Galatians 6:10). I also pray to be on tiptoe all day about giving to those in need and to worthy causes. And mercy? Ah, mercy! I readily admit mercy is not one of my spiritual gifts...but I do pray daily and earnestly for a heart like Jesus' great heart of love, a heart that was moved with compassion when He saw anyone in need.

Dear sister and fellow servant of the Lord, let's seek to serve, give, and show mercy in the way that John Wesley advises—

> Do all the good you can,
> By all the means you can,
> In all the ways you can,
> In all the places you can,
> At all the times you can,
> To all the people you can,
> As long as ever you can.

Some who ministered their gifts—We'll get to what I call "five fat files" in our next chapter, but when I initially set up these five files, one of them was called "The Women of the Bible." In some of these women we witness a variety of ministries being carried out. For instance,

- A band of faithful women ministered their gifts of money and means to help support Jesus and His disciples on their preaching tours (Luke 8:2-3).

- The two sisters Mary and Martha regularly hosted Jesus and his disciples at their home in Bethany (Luke 10:38-39).

- Another faithful group of women remained at the cross, followed those who carried Jesus' body to the tomb, and were the first to arrive in the first rays of daybreak to tend to His corpse, only to be instead the first to learn of His resurrection (Luke 23:49–24:10)!

- The mother of John Mark hosted a prayer meeting at her house...where Peter was prayed out of his cell (Acts 12:12).

211

- The wealthy businesswoman Lydia made her home a gathering place for the believers who made up the budding church at Philippi (Acts 16:40).

- Priscilla, along with her husband, Aquila, ministered personally to Paul (1 Corinthians 16:19) and Apollos, and opened her home for church meetings (Acts 18:24-26).

- Phoebe is described as a servant in her church and a helper of many...including Paul (Romans 16:1-2).

- The widows in the early church dished out not only food and hospitality but a multitude of other good works ranging from raising orphans to nursing the sick (1 Timothy 5:10).

- The older women in the church are to spend their days lovingly teaching and encouraging the younger women (Titus 2:3-5).

What a thrilling parade of female saints! And what did they do? Nothing you and I can't do. They ministered gifts in the areas of service, giving, and mercy. They opened their hearts and handbags and homes to supply help, prayer, assistance, alms, and advice. Again, they did nothing that you and I can't do.

As we close off this section about the array of the spiritual gifts, I just have to share this delightful story. It seems to say it all when it comes to the diversity of spiritual gifts and how they manifest themselves. The illustration centers on a fictitious church dinner where an accident occurs—the cook drops the dessert on the floor! What happens next?

The *server* says, "Here, let me clean it up."

The *leader* says, "Jim, would you go get the mop? Sue, if you will help clean up, Mary and I will fix another dessert."

The *giver* says, "I'll go out and buy another dessert."

The *merciful* says, "Don't feel badly, it could have happened to anyone."

The *prophet* says, "That's what happens when you're not careful."

The *teacher* says, "Clearly, the reason it fell is that it was unbalanced; the tray was too heavy on one side."

The *exhorter* says, "To avoid this in the future, you should use both hands."[1]

Perhaps a good test of your own spiritual giftedness is to ask, "Which one of these responses would I have given?"

Our Growth for Serving the Lord

Now that we know about serving, giving, and mercy, you and I can get busy in our churches. There is nothing that should keep us from following in the footsteps of the inspiring women of the Bible who show us the way to serve the Lord.

But we also have a responsibility to discover, develop, and grow in the use of our primary spiritual gift(s). Many Christians wonder, "How will I know what my gift is? How will I find out my area of giftedness? How will I recognize it?" The following signposts should guide you along the path to discovering your unique giftedness and growing in your service to the Lord and His people.

Your service will bring you joy. Joy is a strong indicator of giftedness. What do you enjoy doing most in ministry, in service to others, in your church?

Your service will bear fruit. When you use your spiritual gifts, others are blessed, and so are you. God's fruit borne through your service is another indicator of your area of giftedness. As you look at your service to others, what does God seem to be blessing most?

Your service will be affirmed by others. As you minister your gifts and others are blessed, they will let you know it. Even if *you* can't put your finger on what you are doing or discern what your gift might be, others can! They will be helped and, believe me, they will express their appreciation! What are others saying to you, thanking you for?

Your service will create opportunities for repeat service. When you minister your gift and grow in your gifted area and others are blessed, chances are you'll be asked again and again to repeat your ministry. What are others asking you to do?

Looking at Life

Serving the Lord! What a vital—and exciting—area this is! And it's truly amazing and humbling to even think that you and I could in *any* way serve God! Yet we are not only commanded to give our lives in service, but we are gifted and enabled by God to serve. As I said, it's truly amazing!

Which leads us to one final guidepost, which sums up not only our ministry in the body of Christ, but the highest passion and purpose any Christian can ever have—

Your service will glorify God. When God's Spirit ministers through you, the Source of your power is obvious to all. It takes on a *supernatural* quality. Why? Because it's not you. It's not natural. And it's not explainable. It's a *spiritual gift*, ministered by the power of the Holy Spirit working in and through you. And ministry done unselfishly and unreservedly in the Spirit will glorify not you, but God...whose we are and whom we serve (Acts 27:23).

Dear one, glorifying God is the purpose of all our service, as it is of all that we say and do in all the areas of our life. As in all other things, our service is to be done *in* the Lord and *unto* the Lord. This combination will ensure that God is glorified! Now,

> As each one has received a gift,
> minister it to one another,
> as good stewards of
> the manifold grace of God...
> that in all things
> God may be glorified
> through Jesus Christ,
> to whom belong the glory
> and the dominion
> forever and ever
> (1 Peter 4:10-11).

Chapter 17

Ten Disciplines
for Managing Your Ministry

As each one has received a gift,
minister it to one another,
as good stewards of the manifold grace of God.
—1 PETER 4:10

In our last chapter I shared how I began ministering and serving the Lord. If you remember, it wasn't very exciting! It all began with answering a form letter that arrived in my mailbox asking for teachers to help start up a women's ministry. As you read my story about stepping across the line and taking the plunge (by faith!) into teaching the Bible, maybe you were thinking, "Well, teaching is definitely not my gift! A public ministry is not for me!"

And you may be right. You may be like the many, many women who responded to the same form letter who volunteered to do a multitude of other ministries that make up the backbone of any Christian endeavor. Some of those dear women volunteered to organize and administrate. Some chose to hostess, to set up, to make or serve the coffee, to type and reproduce the lessons, to sing or lead music, etc.

The point is that we each responded to the call according to our desires for service, our spiritual giftedness, and the prompting of the Holy Spirit. And each response required faith, time, preparation, sacrifice, and a heart to minister.

Are you desiring to serve the Lord, to serve in your church, to serve God's people? I truly hope and pray so, for this is another area of life that needs management. And what I offer here are some of the disciplines that will help you be prepared so that when a letter or a call or an opportunity comes your way, you will be more ready to respond positively...even in the midst of a busy life. Remember... "success" is when our preparation meets God's opportunity!

1. Develop "five fat files."

I often share about the older and wiser woman who said to me early in my Christian life, "Liz, you need five fat files." (And, oh yes, she just happens to be the same wonderful woman who warned me about majoring on the minors!) Anyway, as she talked and I listened and took notes, she expanded on her "five fat files" theory. Literally, it consisted of obtaining five manila file folders, the kind with indentations along the folded end that mark out the file's expansion capacities. So that's Step One—obtain five file folders, which are going to become fat!

After I purchased the folders, I followed Step Two (which, I might add, is vastly more challenging than running into the drug store and grabbing five file folders!). Step Two was to choose five areas for service, or five areas of life, or five subjects in the Bible, where I wanted to purposefully grow. I was to then label each of the folders with one topic. And I now pass that assignment on to you. The reason for limiting yourself to five is to impose some restrictions upon where you put the bulk of your study efforts. You and I cannot be studying everything! So...we choose five subjects.

And, of course, Step Three is to begin filling the files. How? By reading everything you can on your subjects and topics. And not only reading, but recording ideas by outlining, by typing out quotes to save, by jotting down a summary of a book read.

Then there are the classes you take on your subjects, the audiotapes and videotapes you listen to, and the seminars you attend in your five areas. Your handouts and notes from these activities go into the file.

Then add the information you read in magazines, newspapers, or pamphlets. Find a way to copy or clip them, and into the file they go. (And don't forget to take careful notes about the source of the information!)

Then do research, whether from encyclopedias, Bible reference books, the Internet, or the library. Again, record it and file it away in your folders.

And, oh-so-slowly but oh-so-surely, the expansion of your files will indicate that you are reaching expert status! Even with a busy schedule and a hectic life, you will steadily become well-informed on five different vital subjects that speak to the heart and life of Christian women.

Now, what will your five fat files be, dear heart? I'm asking you to take...

Step One—obtain or purchase five manila file folders. Then take...

Step Two—pray...and then select your five ministry topics and label your folders. Don't worry, these subjects are not set in stone. You may change them, and that's okay. But don't let hesitancy or uncertainty be a hindrance to taking Step Two. Then take...

Step Three—begin the exciting adventure of filling your five files until they are fat and filled to overflowing! Just think how much you will be learning! Just think of the growth! And just think of the many women's lives your growth can benefit as your *life* (along with your files) reaches the filled capacity and begins to spill over in ministry! You will never be the same... and neither will the women's lives you touch!

2. Determine your spiritual gifts.

We've already considered many of the scriptures about the spiritual gifts in the body of Christ. And now it's time to seek to discover what your gift(s) might be. Here are a few helps.

- Ask yourself the questions listed in the guidelines for determining what your gifts may be (see the previous chapter under the heading "Our Growth for Serving the Lord").

- Ask other Christians what they see in you, what they see you doing in ministry, how they see you helping others.

- Ask the Lord in prayer to affirm your spiritual gifts.

- Ask your church what needs to be done. Then help out. Once you get busy in your church, you'll begin to find out where "the divine fit" is.

- Look into obtaining a spiritual gifts test or inventory. These tests can help you determine and develop your gifts.

I thank God that I found one of these inventories early in my Christian life. Of all things, it indicated that I had "a measure of faith" (Romans 12:3)! As I looked back through the questions that surfaced this spiritual gift, I gained some idea of what it is faith does and how it manifests itself. Then I turned the questions around and made them into sort of a to do list. For instance, "Those with the gift of faith have an effective prayer ministry." This statement helped me to begin praying for others and to take that ministry of prayer seriously. And here's another one—"Those with the gift of faith are burdened to encourage others to trust God when they are defeated and discouraged." Friend, I believe this outworking of the spiritual gift of faith has come to be the primary emphasis of my ministry to women. Plus knowing this gives me the courage and confidence (in the gift and in the Lord, that is) to speak up when someone is discouraged and share my gift of faith with them. I can only hope and pray that the knowledge of your gifts will spur you on to develop them faithfully and encourage you to use them boldly.

- Ask your heart. I don't think it's wrong to ask your heart what it would like to do to serve God's people. Many times the desire of our hearts (Psalm 37:4) is what leads us straight to our spiritual gifts.

3. Develop your spiritual gifts.

Once you discover areas of giftedness, then you can begin to develop them. And the best way to do that is to read the Bible. The Bible is a spiritual book, and your spiritual gifts are stirred up and empowered as you read God's Word. His

221

Spirit goes to work on your heart, your life, your mind, and your gifts. I find when I'm reading the Bible (and I mean, *as* I'm reading it, right that minute!) ideas for service and ministry come flooding in. People come to mind…and how to minister to them. Needs in the church come to mind…and ideas for meeting those needs.

And this is true for other women too. For instance, I know a woman who is steadily and actively building a "Barnabas ministry" (Acts 4:36-37), a ministry aimed at encouraging people who need encouragement. Another friend of mine operates what I call Judy's Soup Kitchen. A nurse and a two-time survivor of cancer, Judy knows just what's needed when someone is ill. So off she goes with her warm ways, her warm soup, her warm heart brimming over with mercy, and with a heart-warming batch of scriptures to share and leave behind.

So set about to develop your gifts. Faithfully read your Bible and look for references to your gifts, what is taught about them, how they were ministered, and by whom. (And don't forget to save what you discover!)

4. Do pray for ministry opportunities.

Hopefully by now you've set up some kind of prayer notebook. Why not set aside a page to begin praying for opportunities to minister? I've already shared that I pray each and every morning to serve, give, and show mercy "to all the people I can…in all the ways I can." Hurting people are everywhere. Opportunities for ministry, too, are everywhere. Perhaps what we should be praying for are open eyes, open ears, and open hearts (as well as open hands and handbags!). After all, "the eyes of the Lord are on the righteous, and his ears are open to their prayers" (1 Peter 3:12). Shouldn't ours be too?

And while you're praying, pray to be faithful in any ministry you are involved in. Managing ministry is a stewardship…and it is required of a steward that she be found faithful (1 Corinthians 4:2). So pray for faithfulness as you minister out of an already busy life.

5.   Do accept the challenge to grow.

As busy women, our time is always in short supply. But strangely enough, there seems to be enough time to take another trip to the mall or to watch the national average of 6.4 hours of television per day. (And here's another frightening statistic—the average person will spend ten years of their life watching television!) So the issue really isn't the lack of time. No, the issue is the management of our *self.* That's what the author of Hebrews states as he shows his disappointment to his readers concerning their immaturity: "For though by this time you ought to be teachers, you need someone to teach you the first principles of the oracles of God" (Hebrews 5:12). In other words, they had failed to manage their lives in a way that ensured their spiritual growth.

My friend, how long have you been a Christian? That's long enough for you to have learned something that could be passed on to a younger-in-the-Lord sister. The body of Christ needs your gifts. The women in your church need you to be growing so that, if not now then sometime in the future, you have something to pass on. The desperate cry across the country from a new and needy generation of women is, "Where are the older women?" If you and I manage our life with passion and purpose, there *will* be time for us to become the corps of older women who can serve, support, train, and teach our younger sisters.

223

6.   Do allow yourself to be stretched.

Ministry is dynamic. As we accept the challenge to grow spiritually and in our ability to use our gifted areas, more challenging ministries will probably come our way. That's what happened to me. When I took the plunge to teach a Bible class, only six women showed up (and two of them dropped out before the class was over!). Later I was asked to teach an elective workshop...and 60 women showed up (gulp!). Even later, I was invited to teach and lecture, and I found myself in a gymnasium full of women! (Talk about being stretched!)

But many times, that's the way it is when God's people serve Him. For instance, when we first meet Philip in Acts 6, what do we find him doing? He was serving. He was waiting on tables and serving food to the widows in the church (verses 2-5). Then what do we find him doing in Acts 8? He was in Samaria preaching Christ, and the multitudes "heeded the things spoken by Philip, hearing and seeing the miracles which he did" (verse 6). (Talk about being stretched! That's quite a leap—from meals to miracles!)

So, my dear serving friend, do something. Do anything! Just be faithful. Then when other opportunities for ministry come your way, opportunities that promise to stretch you, don't hold back. Instead, look to the Lord for help, be faithful...and let the stretching begin!

7.   Do support others in ministry.

The worst three words in the Bible (in my opinion as a woman) are Paul's words to the leadership at the church in Philippi to "help those women" (Philippians 4:2-3 KJV)! The little book of Philippians is one of the sweetest in the Bible.

It is filled with encouragement and rejoicing as Paul expresses his love for his friends. And then, in the midst of such warmhearted outpourings, Paul has to stop...and name two women...and exhort them to stop bickering and causing trouble...and ask the leaders to help them settle their differences. My response is always as the apostle James exclaimed, "These things ought not to be so" (James 3:10)!

No, they ought not. Instead, we should support others in ministry. You and I know what it takes in time, sacrifice, discipline, preparation, and courage to do *any* ministry. So let's be known as encouragers to all. Let's be the ones who come alongside others who are serving the Lord. Let's be cheerleaders for those who are testing their wings at using their spiritual gifts. Let's volunteer to help them. Let's pray for them. And above all, let's not be critical of them.

8.   Do pray for your pastors and leaders.

One of our greatest ministry contributions can and should be to pray for the leaders of our local churches. These godly leaders serve the church on behalf of Christ and must give an accounting of their faithfulness (Hebrews 13:17). God has given them a high moral standard to live by (1 Timothy 3:1-7; Titus 1:5-9) and they need our constant prayers for moral courage to lead with strength and biblical resolve.

I like James's declaration, "The effective fervent prayer of a righteous man [or woman] avails much" (James 5:16). So make a page in your prayer notebook for your church's leadership, and pray for them on a regular basis. You may want to pick one specific day of the week when you pray for your pastors and leaders. (And P.S., an added benefit of our prayers for our leadership is that we will be less likely to complain or criticize!)

9. Don't neglect your family for ministry.

This point should go without saying…but unfortunately this an area of weakness for many women as the following letter reveals—

> I have been challenged and encouraged by
> God's teaching regarding a woman making
> her family a priority before outside ministry.
> God had been whispering this to me for
> years, but I didn't hear it loud and clear until
> recently. My home is much more peaceful
> now, and I am happier now because my pri-
> orities are more in line with God's priorities.

This is another "bravo" letter! Bravo to this busy wife, mom, and home manager who made the shift and is reaping the blessings of refusing to neglect her family for ministry. (And we can be sure her family is also being blessed!)

Dear reading friend, we must always remember that family *is* a ministry. That biblical teaching must be burned into our hearts and minds. And, at the same time, family is *more than* a ministry. Our family is an assignment from God that He gives to no one else but us. Aside from the ultimate priority we have of nurturing our spiritual life in the Word and in prayer, we have the stewardship—the management— of our marriage, our family, and our home. May we, like the Proverbs 31 woman, ever look well to the ways of our house- hold (Proverbs 31:27)!

Looking at Life

Because this section of each chapter is dedicated to looking at life and our passion for living out God's plan for our lives, this final discipline for managing our ministries seemed to fit here. As you read on, I think you'll agree.

10.   Decide that ministry is for life.

When I think about the span of our lives and life's many varied seasons, an old-fashioned Christian saying seems to hit the mark regarding ministry and life. It says simply that we are "saved to serve." And isn't that the truth? Because we are bought with a price and redeemed by the blood of the Lamb, because we are "saved" out of this world and from our sins, we can "serve" the Lord Christ passionately, gratefully, and humbly...for life!

And while, in the ebb and flow of life, we may experience seasons in our roles and responsibilities, there is no one "season" for service in God's economy. We don't serve until we reach a certain age and then say, "Let someone else do it. I've already put in my time. I've already had my turn. Now it's someone else's time. Let the younger ones take their turn." No, we are saved to serve, or put another way, saved to serve for life. The apostle Paul *pressed on* for the prize (Philippians 3:14) and *fought* a good fight up unto his last dying breath when he *finished* the race (2 Timothy 4:7).

Here's something to think about—my #1 most often asked question is "Where are the older women?" This question is being asked by young women, ranging from high school girls to women into their mid-forties. Each has a unique need for mentoring and teaching and training and is desperately desiring—and asking for—help. But when they step out to follow through on God's instruction to seek instruction from the older women (Titus 2:3-5), they are coming up empty-handed.

Where *are* the older women? Could it be that an attitude of "seasonal" ministry, an attitude of "I've already done my service and put in my time," has taken God's priceless and "seasoned" older women out of the ministry arena so that they are unavailable to the younger women?

As long as you and I have life and breath, God means for us to be involved in ministry. And the older we get, the more we should be able to minister. And the older we get, our ministry should be more meaningful as the years give us greater experience, greater knowledge of the Word, greater wisdom, greater faith, and even greater amounts of time.

So, dear one, let's take God's view of our life and our ministry as our own. Let's decide that ministry is for life. Then let's...

> ...plan for a life of ministry.
> ...prepare for a life of ministry.
> ...pray for a life of ministry.
> ...practice a life of ministry.
> And, by God's grace,
> ...produce a life of ministry.

Part VIII

Managing
Your Time…
and Your Life

Chapter 18

Managing Your Time...
and Your Life

See then that you walk circumspectly, not as fools but as wise,
redeeming the time....Therefore do not be unwise, but
understand what the will of the Lord is.
—EPHESIANS 5:15-17

Well, my faithful traveling companion, we have come full circle in our journey to understanding how to manage our lives as busy women. We started with God and His Word, and we are ending with God and His Word. We started by considering the major areas of our lives with a determination to know God's perspective on these areas. Then we determined, with God's help, to begin to develop the disciplines that better ensure a measure of success in each of these areas. All of this encompasses what the Bible means when it calls you and me to "walk circumspectly, not as fools but as wise...understand[ing] what the will of the Lord is" (Ephesians 5:15,17).

As wise women you and I are to dedicate our lives to knowing and doing God's will. Then, as we seek to do His will, the management of the minutes, the hours, and the days of our lives will come much easier. Why? Because we will be traveling in *God's* direction, toward *God's* will. Instead of struggling against God and His plans and purposes for us, we'll be seeking to do God's work God's way. That's the key to life management, my dear sister—*doing God's work God's way!*

So how do we set about to faithfully accomplish (and with passion and purpose!) all that God is asking of us as His busy women? The Bible gives us the answer—we must *redeem* the time (Ephesians 5:16).

Redeeming Your Time

To redeem your time means to *reclaim, recover, retrieve, rescue,* and *regain* it. And here are a few principles to guide us:

- We redeem time when...we make the most of our *life*, of our limited time on this evil earth, by fulfilling God's purposes. As we line up our *life* and every opportunity for useful worship and service under the will of God, our *life* takes on an extremely efficient quality. We are no longer doing "things." We are no longer governed by the busy-ness of life. We instead begin doing the "*right* things." We begin to focus on doing the business of God. And, dear friend, you will never be too busy *if* you are busy doing the "things" of God!

- We redeem time when...we make the most of our *time*—the minutes, the hours, and the days—of our busy life. As the short-but-sobering poem reminds us,

I have only just a minute,
Only sixty seconds in it...
Just a tiny little minute,
But eternity is in it.

• We redeem time when...we purposefully and prayerfully ask God for His wisdom regarding how we can
  reclaim, recover, retrieve, rescue, and *regain* the minutes, hours, and days of our life for God and His
  glory.

• We redeem time when...we realize that we cannot
  manage time. Time is unmanageable, unrelenting,
  and ever flowing toward eternity. We can only
  manage our *self.* (And that calls for great discipline!)

As we end this book on *Life Management for Busy Women,*
we must look deeply into the mirror of our souls. We must
ask the question, "Do I want to live out God's plan with passion and purpose?" And I know the answer to that question.
It's *yes...yes!...*and a *thousand yeses!* You wouldn't have read
to this point if you weren't ready to do whatever it takes to
understand and begin to fulfill God's will for your life.

So now the question is, *how* do we deal with the time
issue? For most of us, all our good intentions seem to somehow get swallowed up in the swirling whirlwind of our busy
lives. And too often we end up at the end of yet another day
that began with so many wonderful dreams and an equal
number of good intentions, only to find ourselves fully frus-
trated and defeated. We lament with wonder, "What happened?!"

Well, dear one, that's a great question! Go ahead and ask
it. Please! We must always weigh and evaluate the use and

the results of each priceless day. We must always uncover the "time bandits" and the "time robbers" that we are allowing to cheat us out of our valuable minutes. Then, once they are identified, we must guard against them because they can so easily seize our minutes and sap us of our precious life!

Guarding Your Time

To live out God's plan and purposes for your life, you must guard against being robbed of your precious day by time robbers like the ones listed below. Therefore, each evening take some of your valuable time and evaluate the pattern your beautifully planned day took...to see where it went off track. What stole your day away from you? What robbed you of your master plan? Was it...

1. *Procrastination?*—One of the greatest robbers of your time is putting off something you know you should do. Here's the typical scenario: All day long you knew you needed to do something—something important for living out God's plan for your life, something on the high-priority list. Yet for whatever the reason—laziness, fear, lack of follow-up or focus—you failed to finish. Therefore, at day's end, your energy is sapped and your plan for the day is foiled by the task left unfinished. The solution is to determine to put away procrastination. Determine instead to "Do it!" "Just do it!" and "Do it *now!*"

2. *Poor planning and scheduling?*—It's been said, "If you don't plan your day, someone else will plan it for you." So I ask you, who is the best person to plan

your day? Who is it that has prayed through your priorities and desires to do God's will? It's you, dear one! Don't let someone else who is clueless about your goals and your God-given desires and priorities plan your day. It's the day—the only day—God has given you to serve Him. It's all you have for serving Him and for living out His plan...until tomorrow. Don't let someone else have God's day! Instead, plan your day, schedule your day, and protect your day!

3. *People not on the plan for the day?*—As I mentioned in the social section of the book, you and I are social people. We love people and love to be with them. And this is as it should be. But you must determine how much of God's time and day you can give to people. There are, of course, the priority people in your life—your family—who must be given as much time as they need. (After all, your family is the masterpiece you are assigned by God to create.) But beyond these loved ones you are to be discerning. With each encounter you must learn to ask God for wisdom. You must go to the Father of time and ask Him how much time should be spent with each person. Ask Him to spell out what the need of the moment is...and then follow His leading. So determine to pray as interruptions come up!

4. *Poor delegation?*—As a wife and mother there aren't many people in your life that you can delegate to. You can't delegate to your three-year-old...but you can definitely delegate to your 13-year-old! So be sure you instill responsibility in your children as they grow up. (And the earlier the better!) It will develop

character in their lives and lighten your load. And it will make living in your family a team effort. More work will get done as others assist you, and you will get the things done that only you can do.

5. *Poor use of the telephone?*—The telephone is a marvelous assistant and time management tool. For instance, instead of running all over town to find something, you can "let your fingers do the walking." But you must discipline yourself to safeguard against wasting your precious time by getting on and off the phone as quickly as possible. And here's another discipline—jot down everything you want to cover in your conversation before you make the call. Plus (it goes without saying...almost) completely cut out the use of your phone as an instrument for spreading malicious gossip and being "busybodies, saying things which they ought not" (1 Timothy 5:13). Destroying the character of others is never a part of God's plan! Instead use the telephone to better the lives of all. Don't let your *phone* master you. Instead, *you* master your phone.

6. *Poring over junk mail and newspapers?*—Have you ever seen a real newspaper junkie? They're the person who methodically and carefully reads every item in the paper...including the obituaries. They are very adroit at folding the paper so as to create the neatest of reading surfaces. They spend hours poring over the pages of the paper. And junk mail addicts are no different. They stop everything when the mail arrives to spend large amounts of their precious time and energy poring over each and every

piece of paper that comes in the mail. True, there is some value in being current on the news, clipping coupons, and looking for sale items. But be on guard to make sure these secondary things don't rob you of time for the good, the better, the best, and the eternal. Put these activities in their rightful place— at the end of your day (if at all!), at the time when your energy level nears zero. (Or you can put them in the trash can.) Make it a discipline not to spend more time on newspapers and junk mail than you spend on spiritual matters like reading your Bible, memorizing Scripture, and praying.

7. *Priorities out of whack?*—Many times the biggest time robber of all is the mismanagement of our priorities. We've already determined that we are busy women. Just one glance at your schedule and this busy-ness is very evident! But busy-ness is not an indicator of effectiveness. If you and I are busy doing the wrong things, then we are being robbed of time that could be better spent on the things that truly count—our God-given priorities. That's why it's so important to take time each day to go through these exercises for redeeming your time and guarding your time.

Now, my dear and beloved friend and journey's companion, it's time to part ways and go the journey alone. But I ask one more thing of you as you go on to manage your busy life for the Lord—follow the prayer guide on page 239 for living out God's plan. I think (and hope...and pray!) that as you pray and plan and prepare to live out God's plan for the remaining days of your life, you'll find yourself taking flight in God's direction. You'll surprise yourself as you mount up with wings as an eagle, as you run and are not weary, as you walk and do not faint (Isaiah 40:31). You'll discover the power of eagles' wings lifting you, sustaining you, and carrying you along in making your dream for a life lived in the center of God's will a reality. And the passion? The passion, too, will mount...and mount...and mount... until the sublime passion to live out God's plan for your life is all-consuming.

Pray, dear precious one! Pray the prayer that follows on page 239. Pray it each day. Pray it throughout the day. Pray it at the end of your day. And pray it every day. Then live out each day with all your might. And may each and every one of them be blessed by delightful fellowship with Your heavenly Father along the way.

A Prayer for Living Out God's Plan

1. *Pray over your priorities*—"Lord, what is Your will for me at this time in my life?"

2. *Plan through your priorities*—"Lord, what must I do today to accomplish Your will?"

3. *Prepare a schedule based on your priorities*—"Lord, when should I do the things that live out these priorities today?"

4. *Proceed to implement your priorities*—"Lord, thank You for giving me Your direction for my day."

5. *Purpose to check your progress*—"Lord, I only have a limited time left in my day. What important tasks do I need to focus on for the remainder of the day?"

6. *Prepare for tomorrow*—"Lord, how can I better live out Your plan for my life tomorrow?"

7. *Praise God at the end of the day*—"Lord, thank You for a meaningful day, for 'a day well spent,' for I have offered my life and this day to You as a 'living sacrifice.'"

QUIET TIMES CALENDAR

Jan.	Feb.	Mar.	Apr.	May	June
1	1	1	1	1	1
2	2	2	2	2	2
3	3	3	3	3	3
4	4	4	4	4	4
5	5	5	5	5	5
6	6	6	6	6	6
7	7	7	7	7	7
8	8	8	8	8	8
9	9	9	9	9	9
10	10	10	10	10	10
11	11	11	11	11	11
12	12	12	12	12	12
13	13	13	13	13	13
14	14	14	14	14	14
15	15	15	15	15	15
16	16	16	16	16	16
17	17	17	17	17	17
18	18	18	18	18	18
19	19	19	19	19	19
20	20	20	20	20	20
21	21	21	21	21	21
22	22	22	22	22	22
23	23	23	23	23	23
24	24	24	24	24	24
25	25	25	25	25	25
26	26	26	26	26	26
27	27	27	27	27	27
28	28	28	28	28	28
29		29	29	29	29
30		30	30	30	30
31		31		31	

DATE BEGUN _____

July	Aug.	Sept.	Oct.	Nov.	Dec.
1	1	1	1	1	1
2	2	2	2	2	2
3	3	3	3	3	3
4	4	4	4	4	4
5	5	5	5	5	5
6	6	6	6	6	6
7	7	7	7	7	7
8	8	8	8	8	8
9	9	9	9	9	9
10	10	10	10	10	10
11	11	11	11	11	11
12	12	12	12	12	12
13	13	13	13	13	13
14	14	14	14	14	14
15	15	15	15	15	15
16	16	16	16	16	16
17	17	17	17	17	17
18	18	18	18	18	18
19	19	19	19	19	19
20	20	20	20	20	20
21	21	21	21	21	21
22	22	22	22	22	22
23	23	23	23	23	23
24	24	24	24	24	24
25	25	25	25	25	25
26	26	26	26	26	26
27	27	27	27	27	27
28	28	28	28	28	28
29	29	29	29	29	29
30	30	30	30	30	30
31	31		31		31

If you have enjoyed the truths and principles shared in this book, you will also benefit from its companion volume, *Life Management for Busy Women Growth and Study Guide.*

Notes

Chapter 1—Developing a Passion for God's Word

1. Curtis Vaughan, *The Old Testament Books of Poetry from 26 Translations*, quoting The Jerusalem Bible (Grand Rapids: Zondervan Bible Publishers, 1973), p. 144.

2. D. L. Moody, *Notes from My Bible and Thoughts from My Library*, slightly adapted (Grand Rapids: Baker Book House, 1979), p. 110.

3. Albert M. Wells, Jr., *Inspiring Quotations—Contemporary & Classical* (Nashville: Thomas Nelson Publishers, 1988), p. 15.

4. Ibid., p. 13.

Chapter 2—Ten Disciplines for Developing a Passion for God's Word

1. Sherwood Eliot Wirt and Kersten Beckstrom, eds., *Topical Encyclopedia of Living Quotations*, quoting Gladys Brooks (Minneapolis: Bethany House Publishers, 1982), p. 57.

2. J. Oswald Sanders, *Spiritual Leadership* (Chicago: Moody Press, 1980), p. 54.

3. Frank S. Mead, *12,000 Religious Quotations* (Grand Rapids: Baker Book House, 2000), p. 32.

4. Arnold A. Dallimore, *Susanna Wesley, the Mother of John and Charles Wesley* (Grand Rapids: Baker Book House, 1994), p. 15.

5. Edith Schaeffer, *Common Sense Christian Living* (Nashville: Thomas Nelson Publishers, 1983), p. 209.

6. The Tract League, Grand Rapids, MI 49544-1390.

Chapter 3—Developing a Passion for Prayer

1. Terry W. Glaspey, *Pathway to the Heart of God* (Eugene, OR: Harvest House Publishers, 1998), p. 24.

2. Donald S. Whitney, *Ten Questions to Diagnose Your Spiritual Health* (Colorado Springs: NavPress, 2001), pp. 92-93.

3. Elizabeth George, *A Woman After God's Own Heart* (Eugene, OR: Harvest House Publishers, 1997), p. 36.

4. Herbert Lockyer, *All the Prayers of the Bible* (Grand Rapids: Zondervan Publishing House, 1984), p. 73.

5. W. L. Doughty, ed., *The Prayers of Susanna Wesley* (Grand Rapids: Zondervan Publishing House, 1984).

6. Ibid., pp. 39, 46.

Chapter 4—God's Guidelines for Your Body

1. Frank S. Mead, ed., *12,000 Religious Quotations*, quoting Charles Haddon Spurgeon (Grand Rapids: Baker Book House, 2000), p. 228.

2. Albert M. Wells, Jr., ed., *Inspiring Quotations—Contemporary & Classical*, quoting Wendell W. Price (Nashville: Thomas Nelson Publishers, 1988), p. 179.

3. *Life Application Bible Commentary—1 & 2 Corinthians*, quoting Gordon Fee (Wheaton, IL: Tyndale House Publishers, Inc., 1999), p. 88.

4. Robert Boyd Munger, *My Heart, Christ's Home* (Downers Grove, IL: InterVarsity Christian Fellowship, 1986).

5. Sid Buzzell, gen. ed., *The Leadership Bible* (Grand Rapids: Zondervan Publishing House, 1998), p. 1344.

Chapter 5—Ten Disciplines for Managing Your Body, Part 1

1. John MacArthur, *The MacArthur Study Bible* (Nashville: Word Publishing, 1997), p. 1981.

2. Curtis Vaughan, ed., *The New Testament from 26 Translations* (Grand Rapids: Zondervan Publishing House, 1967), p. 744.

3. D. L. Moody, *Notes from My Bible and Thoughts from My Library* (Grand Rapids: Baker Book House, 1979), p. 159.

4. Elizabeth George, *Beautiful in God's Eyes—The Treasures of the Proverbs 31 Woman* (Eugene, OR: Harvest House Publishers, 1998).

Chapter 6—Ten Disciplines for Managing Your Body, Part 2

1. Elisabeth Elliot, *Discipline, the Glad Surrender* (Grand Rapids: Fleming H. Revell, 1982), pp. 46-47.

2. E. C. McKenzie, *Mac's Giant Book of Quips & Quotes* (Grand Rapids, MI: Baker Books, 1980), p. 165.

3. Peter Drucker, *The Effective Executive* (New York: Harper Business Books, 1996), p. 549.

4. J. Oswald Sanders, *Spiritual Leadership* (Chicago: Moody Press, 1980).

5. John Maxwell, *The 21 Indispensable Qualities of a Leader* (Nashville: Thomas Nelson Publishers, 1999), p. 128.

A Word of Testimony

1. Elizabeth George, *A Woman After God's Own Heart, Beautiful in God's Eyes, A Woman's High Calling* (Eugene, OR: Harvest House Publishers).

Chapter 7—Managing Your Marriage

1. D. Edmond Hiebert, *Everyman's Bible Commentary—Titus and Philemon* (Chicago: Moody Press, 1957), p. 50.

2. Adapted from Roy B. Zuck, *The Speaker's Quote Book* (Grand Rapids: Kregel Publications, 1997), p. 242.

3. Zuck, *The Speaker's Quote Book,* p. 242.

Chapter 8—Managing Your Children

1. William MacDonald, *Enjoying the Proverbs* (Walterick Publishers, P.O. Box 2216, Kansas City, KS 66110), p. 120.

2. D. Edmond Hiebert, *Everyman's Bible Commentary—Titus and Philemon* (Chicago: Moody Press, 1957), p. 50.

3. *The Honolulu Advertiser,* January 27, 2000.

4. Howard G. Hendricks, "God's Blueprint for Family Living" (Lincoln, NE: Back to the Bible, 1976), pp. 44-56.

Chapter 9—Managing Your Home

1. Curtis Vaughan, *The Old Testament Books of Poetry from 26 Translations* (Grand Rapids: Zondervan Publishing House, 1967), p. 1017.

2. Emilie Barnes, *Simply Organized* (Eugene, OR: Harvest House Publishers, 1997).

Chapter 10—God's Guidelines for Your Money

1. Frank S. Mead, *12,000 Religious Quotations,* quoting George Chapman, "The Tears of Peace" (Grand Rapids: Baker Book House, 1989), p. 87.

2. Ibid., p. 311.

3. Albert M. Wells, Jr., *Inspiring Quotations—Contemporary & Classical,* quoting Johann Wolfgang von Goethe (Nashville: Thomas Nelson Publishers, 1988), p. 49.

4. Jeremiah Burroughs, *The Rare Jewel of Christian Contentment* (Carlisle, PA: The Banner of Truth Trust, 2000).

5. Helen H. Lemmel, "Turn Your Eyes Upon Jesus," public domain.

Chapter 11—Ten Disciplines for Managing Your Money

1. Summarized from J. Allan Petersen, *For Men Only,* quoting from "Changing Times," the Kiplinger Magazine, February 1969 issue (Wheaton, IL: Tyndale House Publishers, 1974), pp. 155-57.

2. Curtis Vaughan, *The New Testament from 26 Translations,* quoting The New Testament in Modern English (Grand Rapids: Zondervan Publishing House, 1967), p. 826.

3. Frank S. Mead, *12,000 Religious Quotations,* quoting Oliver Wendell Holmes, Sr., (Grand Rapids: Baker Book House, 2000), p. 310.

Chapter 12—God's Guidelines for Your Friendships

1. Jim and Elizabeth George, *God's Wisdom for Little Girls* and *God's Wisdom for Little Boys* (Eugene, OR: Harvest House Publishers, 2000 and 2002, respectively).

2. Frank S. Mead, *12,000 Religious Quotations* (Grand Rapids: Baker Book House, 2000), p. 155.

3. Ibid., quoting Joseph Addison's *The Campaign*, p. 154.

4. Kent Hughes, *Disciplines of a Godly Man* (Wheaton, IL: Crossway Books, 1991), pp. 62-63.

5. Frank S. Mead, *12,000 Religious Quotations*, anonymous, p. 154.

Chapter 13—Ten Disciplines for Managing Your Friendships ˙

1. Curtis Vaughan, *The Old Testament Books of Poetry from 26 Translations* (Grand Rapids: Zondervan Bible Publishers, 1973), pp. 234-35.

2. Frank S. Mead, *12,000 Religious Quotation* (Grand Rapids: Baker Book House, 2000), p. 155.

3. Curtis Vaughan, *The New Testament from 26 Translations* (Grand Rapids: Zondervan Publishing House, 1967), p. 771.

4. Mead, *12,000 Religious Quotations*, quoting Hovey, p. 156.

5. Anne Ortlund, *Building a Great Marriage* (Old Tappan, NJ: Fleming H. Revell Company, 1984), p. 155.

6. Albert M. Wells, Jr., *Inspiring Quotations—Contemporary & Classical* (Nashville: Thomas Nelson Publishers, 1988), p. 176.

7. Roy B. Zuck, *The Speaker's Quote Book* (Grand Rapids: Kregel Publications, 1997), p. 159.

Chapter 14—God's Guidelines for Your Mind

1. D.L. Moody, *Notes from My Bible and Thoughts from My Library*, quoting McKenzie (Grand Rapids: Baker Book House, 1979), pp. 318-19.

2. Warren W. Wiersbe, *Be Joyful* (Wheaton, IL: Victor Books, 1979), p. 116.

3. Roy B. Zuck, *The Speaker's Quote Book* (Grand Rapids: Kregel Publications, 1997), p. 383.

Chapter 15—Ten Disciplines for Managing Your Mind

1. Sherwood Eliot Wirt and Kersten Beckstrom, eds., *Topical Encyclopedia of Living Quotations*, quoting Charles F. Kettering (Minneapolis: Bethany House Publishers, 1982), p. 83.

2. J. Oswald Sanders, *Spiritual Leadership* (Chicago: Moody Press, 1980), p. 149.

3. Moody Correspondence School, 820 North LaSalle Street, Chicago, IL 60610, 1-800-621-7105.

Chapter 16—God's Guidelines for Your Ministry

1. Mark Porter, *The Time of Your Life*, citing Bill Gothard and the Institute of Basic Youth Conflicts (Wheaton, IL: Victor Books, 1983), pp. 70-71.

Personal Notes

Personal Notes

Personal Notes

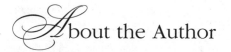

About the Author

Elizabeth George is a bestselling author and speaker whose passion is to teach the Bible in a way that changes women's lives. For information about Elizabeth's books or speaking ministry, to sign up for her mailings, or to share how God has used this book in your life, please write to Elizabeth at:

Elizabeth George
P.O. Box 2879
Belfair, WA 98528

Toll-free fax/phone: 1-800-542-4611
www.elizabethgeorge.com

≈

Books by Elizabeth George

Beautiful in God's Eyes—The Treasures of the Proverbs 31 Woman
Life Management for Busy Women
Life Management for Busy Women Growth and Study Guide
The Lord Is My Shepherd—12 Promises for Every Woman
Loving God with All Your Mind
A Woman After God's Own Heart®
A Woman After God's Own Heart® Audiobook
A Woman After God's Own Heart® Growth and Study Guide
A Woman After God's Own Heart® Prayer Journal
Women Who Loved God—365 Days with the Women of the Bible
A Woman's High Calling—10 Essentials for Godly Living
A Woman's High Calling Growth and Study Guide
A Woman's Walk with God—Growing in the Fruit of the Spirit
A Woman's Walk with God Growth and Study Guide

A Woman After God's Own Heart® Bible Study Series
Walking in God's Promises—The Life of Sarah
Cultivating a Life of Character—Judges/Ruth
Becoming a Woman of Beauty & Strength—Esther
Nurturing a Heart of Humility—The Life of Mary
Experiencing God's Peace—Philippians
Pursuing Godliness—1 Timothy
Growing in Wisdom & Faith—James
Putting On a Gentle & Quiet Spirit—1 Peter

Children's Books
God's Wisdom for Little Boys—Character-Building Fun from Proverbs
(co-authored with Jim George)
God's Wisdom for Little Girls—Virtues & Fun from Proverbs 31
God's Little Girl Is Helpful
God's Little Girl Is Kind